'I am always at a banquet when I hear Mark teaching. This book will inspire and equip all teachers of the Bible to be more effective.'

J. John, author and evangelist

'A fresh, insightful approach to an often neglected topic. Mark's insights are particularly useful to the emerging generation of leaders and all those who desire to teach the Word of God.'

Dr Martin Sanders, Professor of Preaching, Nyack Theological Seminary, New York

'An anointed preacher and teacher who believes in a Word and Spirit ministry, accomplishing his inspired work in print.'

David Shearman, Pastor of Assemblies of God, Talbot Street, Nottingham

'This is Mark Stibbe at his best. Every minister and church leader should read it.'

R. T. Kendall, former Minister of Westminster Chapel, London

This book is dedicated to Dr R.T. Kendall,
a man of the Spirit and the word
and an inspiration to Bible teachers everywhere.

The Teacher's Notebook

MARK STIBBE

KINGSWAY PUBLICATIONS
EASTBOURNE

Unless otherwise indicated, biblical quotations are from the
New Living Translation copyright © 1996 by Tyndale Charitable Trust.
Used by permission of Tyndale House Publishers, Wheaton, Illinois, USA.
AV = Authorised Version (King James) Crown copyright.
NIV = New International Version © 1973, 1978, 1984 by the
    International Bible Society.
RSV = Revised Standard Version, copyright © 1946, 1952, 1971, 1973 by
    the Division of Christian Education of the National Council of
    the Churches of Christ in the USA.
TLB = The Living Bible © Tyndale House Publishers 1971.

ISBN 1 84291 003 5

Published by
KINGSWAY COMMUNICATIONS LTD
Lottbridge Drove, Eastbourne BN23 6NT, England.
Email: books@kingsway.co.uk

Book design and production for the publishers by
Bookprint Creative Services, P.O. Box 827, BN21 3YJ, England.
Printed in Great Britain.

Contents

	Acknowledgements	7
1.	Introducing the Gift	9
2.	Learning from Jesus	37
3.	Ministering with Power	62
4.	Expounding the Bible	90
5.	Preparing the Message	121
	Conclusion: Leaving a Legacy	148

Acknowledgements

I would like to express my thanks to my wife Alie and to my friend J. John for reading the manuscript carefully and suggesting helpful refinements.

I owe a great debt of thanks to Phil and Helen Clark and all those at St Andrew's who were praying for me as I wrote this book, particularly in the latter stages.

Thanks are due also to Barry Kissell for inviting me to take part in this project and to Richard Herkes for his patience with me.

I am grateful to all those men and women of the Spirit and the word who have been an inspiration to me in the ministry of Bible teaching, and I am likewise grateful to all the people I teach week in, week out at St Andrew's for their equally inspirational encouragement.

Thanks to all those whose wise sayings I have quoted in this book, both living and departed. Some of these quotes do not have specific references, I am afraid. I have simply picked them up over the years from other speakers, or over the Internet.

Finally, thanks to the New Living Translation. I have used this excellent contemporary version of the Bible throughout, except where I indicate otherwise.

1

Introducing the Gift

My school days were over a long time ago. And yet I still have very vivid memories of those who taught me well. I remember Guy Gross, who taught me maths. I remember Trevor Park, who taught me English literature. I remember Geoff Hewitson, who coached and trained me to excel at sport. These people left an indelible impression on my life. Much of what I am today I owe to these important figures in my past. As William Arthur Ward once wrote:

> The mediocre teacher tells
> The good teacher explains
> The superior teacher demonstrates
> The great teacher inspires

These teachers *inspired* me.

As a Christian, I feel the same way about certain people who have been inspirational teachers in the church. There are a number who have had a very special gift in this particular 'pulpit' ministry. People like David Shearman, a fervent Pentecostal pastor, who has never failed to make the Bible fresh, relevant and life-changing. People like

John Wimber, whose teaching about the kingdom of God completely revolutionised my thinking and my ministry. People like R. T. Kendall, who has always had a wonderful ability to expound the word in the power of the Spirit. People like J. John, arguably the finest preacher of the gospel in the UK today and a real example to all those who aspire to be effective communicators. These people have had an immense impact on my life. As Bible teachers, they have been an inspirational example to me personally.

This book is about the spiritual gift of teaching. It is a practical handbook for those who are training to become teachers, or those who are already practitioners. My prayer is that this will, by the grace of God, prove inspirational to you.

Back to the first century

Before we can appreciate the importance of Bible teaching in today's church, we need to travel back in time to the first century AD and see how important this ministry was then.

Jesus was called 'Teacher' and those who heard him were astonished by his ability to communicate truths about the kingdom of God. At the end of his time on earth, Jesus commissioned his followers to go and make disciples of all nations, telling them – among other things – to *teach* new converts (Matthew 28:18–20). After the watershed experience of the Day of Pentecost, we find the earliest followers of Jesus 'devoted to the apostles' teaching' (Acts 2:42). In Paul's letters we find references to the ministry of the teacher in the earliest churches, and there is also mention in his letters of 'the gift of teaching'. Clearly, the gift of teaching was exercised by Jesus, by the disciples, by Paul and by the Spirit-filled churches of the first century AD.

Why was the teaching ministry so important to the early church? It is to Paul's letters that we must turn if we are to answer this question. His first reference to 'teaching' or 'teachers' is in 1 Corinthians 12. In this chapter about the gifts of the Spirit, Paul concludes by stressing that not everyone has the same God-given ability. There is unity in the church, yes, but there is not uniformity. In fact, God has graciously given a diversity of gifts to his people. So Paul says in verses 27–28:

> Now all of you together are Christ's body, and each one of you is a separate and necessary part of it. Here is a list of some of the members that God has placed in the body of Christ: first are apostles, second are prophets, third are teachers, then those who do miracles, those who have the gift of healing, those who can help others, those who can get others to work together, those who speak in unknown languages.

Notice the word 'teachers' here. Clearly, there were some in the church at Corinth who were set apart as teachers and whose role was critical enough to merit third place in the list above. This special role of 'the teacher' was given to some but not to all. This is why Paul continues in verses 29–30:

> Is everyone an apostle? Of course not. Is everyone a prophet? No. Are all teachers? Does everyone have the power to do miracles? Does everyone have the gift of healing? Of course not.

Elsewhere in 1 Corinthians Paul reveals what happened when the church in Corinth met to worship the Lord. So he writes in 1 Corinthians 14:26:

Well, my brothers and sisters, let's summarize what I am saying. When you meet, one will sing, another will teach, another will share some special revelation God has given, one will speak in an unknown language, while another will interpret what is said.

Here we see that teaching (*didache* is the Greek word) was an important part of 'charismatic' or Spirit-inspired worship.

Moving on to the book of Romans, it is important to note how Paul includes 'teaching' in the list of the spiritual gifts in 12:6–8:

God has given each of us the ability to do certain things well. So if God has given you the ability to prophesy, speak out when you have faith that God is speaking through you. If your gift is that of serving others, serve them well. If you are a teacher, do a good job of teaching. If your gift is to encourage others, do it! If you have money, share it generously. If God has given you leadership ability, take the responsibility seriously. And if you have a gift for showing kindness to others, do it gladly.

By the time we get to Ephesians, Paul can say of the ascended Lord Jesus: 'He is the one who gave these gifts to the church: the apostles, the prophets, the evangelists, and the pastors and teachers' (Ephesians 4:11).

Much has been written about the word 'and' in that last phrase. Is the 'and' meant to suggest that Paul is in fact referring to one gift, that of the 'pastor–teacher'? Or is it simply there to conclude a sequence of thought? Some think the writer uses it in order to suggest that there is in fact one gift, the gift of being a pastor-and-teacher. This would make four ministries rather than five in Ephesians

4:11. Others think that it is used to highlight the fact that the list is ending, so that there are in fact two gifts, pastor and teacher. This preserves the conventional perspective of five rather than four ministries (and also justifies the writing of this present volume!).

I personally believe that the best way to read 'pastors and teachers' is as separate gifts. The original Greek suggests that Paul uses the word 'and' purely and simply to conclude a list (much as we would place 'and' before the final item in a list in English). At the same time, it is not unimportant that Paul puts these two ministries side by side in his sentence. The word 'pastor' literally means a shepherd. A shepherd is someone who knows the sheep. The teacher, on the other hand, is someone who feeds the sheep. When we put it like this, a pastor has to be able to teach and a teacher has to be able to pastor. A pastor cannot look after the sheep without at least some feeding or teaching ministry. A teacher cannot feed the sheep without at least some contact with them of a pastoral kind. It therefore makes sense for Paul to link the two ministries so closely together.

Putting all the data together, we can summarise the evidence of the New Testament as follows:

1. Jesus was an inspirational teacher.
2. He called his closest followers to teach others.
3. After Pentecost, God gave the gift of teaching to his church.
4. Those who excelled in this gift became teachers.
5. Teaching was a key ingredient in Spirit-filled worship.

A God-given ability

What, then, is the gift of teaching? I define it as 'the God-given ability to instruct believers in a biblical and a revelatory way'.

Let's take the first part of this definition – 'a God-given ability'. It is extremely important for us to understand that the gifts of the Spirit are not natural talents or the result of human training but rather divine endowments. When the apostle Paul speaks of the teacher in Ephesians 4:11 he speaks of a person gifted by the Lord of heaven. When he speaks about teaching in Romans 12:6–7 he stresses that it is God who has given us the ability to do certain things well. In fact, he uses a very distinctive word to describe these God-given abilities, the word *charisma* in Greek (*charismata* in the plural). This word is probably something that Paul coined under the inspiration of the Holy Spirit. In creating this term, Paul emphasises that the gifts of the Spirit have their source in the *charis* or grace of God. The gift of teaching – like all the gifts – is the result of the lavish love of the Lord. Though we may have the predisposition, the personality and the passion for teaching, this gift is the result of God's power, not of our profile. While schoolteachers and university lecturers may have a natural aptitude for educating others, Bible teachers are gifted by the Spirit.

To emphasise the point, I would like to share a brief testimony about the beginning of my own ministry as a teacher in the church. I still remember it very vividly. I was sitting in an auditorium in Sheffield city centre. It was the last morning of a four-day conference with the American church leader John Wimber. The year was 1985. There were several thousand delegates present.

It had been an extremely powerful week. I had arrived

somewhat apprehensive on the Monday for the start of the conference. I had heard much about John Wimber's teaching on the Holy Spirit and particularly about his views concerning miracles. I had also heard about the extraordinary manifestations of God's power that had accompanied his teaching ministry, both in his home church in California, and on his travels during conferences. Stories of people weeping, laughing, shaking, prophesying or being healed were commonplace. Part of me was sceptical. Part of me was desperately hungry for more of God.

By the Thursday morning, it seemed that every delegate had been touched except me. I was not particularly looking for anything physical. But I was eagerly seeking the Father's presence in my life, and at least some sense of him speaking to me. Up until the last session of the conference, this had not happened and I was beginning to feel very left out. Now it was Thursday morning, and my friends and I were within an hour of returning home.

During the final moments of the final session, John Wimber stood up and told us that he had sensed a word from the Lord. He believed that the Father wanted to equip people for what he called the fivefold ministries. Now I have to admit that I had never heard that phrase before, so I was glad that John (as always) was sensitive to people's need for further explanation. He read out the passage in Ephesians chapter 4 where the writer tells us how the ascended Lord Jesus gave gifts to his church. John Wimber pointed to the five ministries in verse 11: apostles, prophets, evangelists, pastors and teachers. He then started to pray that the Lord Jesus would release each of these ministries in his church today.

I waited with my hands and heart open to receive from

the Lord. John spoke the word 'apostles', and then asked the Father to anoint those called to apostleship. After some minutes of extraordinary scenes, he went on to the word 'prophets' and did the same. Once again, there was a visible response. He went on to 'evangelists'. Similar things happened. He mentioned 'pastors'. More people responded. Finally, he mentioned the word 'teachers', and something unusual began to happen to me.

There are some moments in your Christian life that are simply life-changing. This was one of them. As John mentioned the word 'teachers', my right hand began to shake. I remember sitting and watching this with amazement. There was absolutely no way that I was doing this myself.

As my right hand shook more intensely, I began to feel curious. I suppose it is the theologian in me, but I started to ask the question, 'What does this experience mean?' John Wimber had taught us always to ask the question, 'Father, what are you doing?' As I asked this, I sensed him asking *me* a question. Now this was not an audible voice. It was more like the inner impression of a voice. He asked, 'What is the one thing you can do with your right hand that you cannot do with your left?' I said, 'Write.' And then I sensed the Father saying words that have shaped my destiny since that day: 'Yes, and I am calling you to be a writer and a teacher in my kingdom. You will write about renewal and revival and you will teach the word of God in the power of the Spirit.'

And that was it. My hand stopped shaking. I left the auditorium a few minutes later and travelled home. But nothing would ever be the same.

Now I do not mean to suggest that you have to experience a shaking hand and a prophetic word in order to become a teacher in the church! That would of course be foolish. The reason I tell this story is simply to underline the point that teaching is a God-given ability. It is 'charismatic' in the root sense of the word. It is an example of extraordinary favour given to ordinary people. While it is true that I already had something of a natural aptitude for public speaking, not to mention theological training, I do not regard either of these things as the source of the teaching ministry I now exercise. Rather, I regard the John Wimber conference in 1985 as the moment when the Father gave an undeserving son a special grace. The source of whatever teaching and writing ability I have is in the *grace* of God, not the expertise of human beings.

So, let me stress: the gift of teaching is a God-given ability. As with all the gifts, we should always acknowledge, thank and honour the Giver. The ministries of the apostle, the prophet, the evangelist, the pastor and the teacher are heavenly blessings given to the church on earth.

Instructing believers

The second part of my definition stresses that the teaching gift is given for the purpose of 'instructing believers'. In other words, the teacher's target audience is those who have already given their lives to the Lord Jesus and who desire to learn more.

It is really important at this point that we understand the difference between the evangelist and the teacher. Broadly speaking, the evangelist preaches the gospel to unbelievers, while teachers expound the Bible to believers. Evangelists bring people in. Teachers bring people on.

For a long time the differences between these two ministries have been explained using the two Greek words *kerygma* and *didache*. *Kerygma* refers to the act of preaching the gospel, and also to the content of the gospel – the good news of the kingdom of God. Thus, Paul can say, 'Since God in his wisdom saw to it that the world would never find him through human wisdom, he has used our foolish preaching [*kerygma*] to save all who believe' (1 Corinthians 1:21). Here, *kerygma* very clearly refers to preaching the gospel to the lost.

On the other hand, when Paul uses *didache* it usually refers to teaching believers, not preaching to unbelievers. Thus, Paul writes in 1 Corinthians 14:6:

> Dear brothers and sisters, if I should come to you talking in an unknown language, how would that help you? But if I bring you some revelation or some special knowledge or some prophecy or some teaching [*didache*] – that is what will help you.

This popular distinction between *kerygma* and *didache*, between preaching and teaching, is helpful. In the most thorough study of these words to date, James McDonald writes: 'that there is a broad distinction between preaching and teaching, in the ancient and the modern world, must be allowed.'[1] However, McDonald also points out that we should not push the differences too far. Whenever people teach doctrine, that doctrine is thoroughly rooted in the gospel of Jesus Christ. *Didache*, in other words, flows out of *kerygma*. Similarly, there is clear evidence in the New Testament that people taught believers by reminding them of the *kerygma*.

---

[1] James McDonald, *Kerygma and Didache* (Cambridge: Cambridge University Press, 1980), p. 5.

Now I appreciate that the discussion at this point is quite technical, but it is relevant to our subject. The fact is: the person who has the God-given ability to teach will primarily be involved in *instructing believers*. This will be their 'base' or 'normal' ministry. They may at times find themselves preaching the gospel to unbelievers, but this will be their 'phase' or 'occasional' ministry.[2]

So, for example, my base ministry is teaching. The thing that I love to do, and have the opportunity to do, is to expound the word of God in the power of the Spirit, and this to believers. Although I have to work hard in preparation, although I exert great energy in the delivery of a message, the task of teaching is not a difficult one for me. It feels supernaturally natural, to use John Wimber's very helpful phrase.

From time to time, however, I find myself in situations where I am with an audience of unbelievers, perhaps at a guest service, or at a meal. In these situations, I switch from my base ministry of teaching to my phase ministry of evangelism. I move from *teaching* to *preaching*. Here, I find I have to work far harder in my preparation. It is not so 'supernaturally natural' for me to communicate with groups and crowds of unbelievers. Friends of mine, like J. John, excel at this kind of thing because it is their base rather than their phase ministry. Though it requires hard work, for them it feels almost effortless when they are in full flow. Their base ministry is as the evangelist, whereas mine is as the teacher. They love preaching while I love teaching. Jesus, of course, could switch from teaching to preaching with consummate ease. As Matthew reports

---

[2] For more on 'base' and 'phase' ministries, see Mike Breen's *The Apostle's Notebook* (Kingsway, 2002), pp. 172–192.

(4:23): 'Jesus travelled throughout Galilee *teaching* in the synagogues, *preaching* everywhere the Good News about the Kingdom' (my italics).

While there is evidently a degree of overlap between teaching and preaching, the following summary is still helpful in clarifying the main differences between the two:

	AUDIENCE	GIFT/MINISTRY	PURPOSE
PREACHING	Unbelievers	Evangelist	Salvation
TEACHING	Believers	Teacher	Sanctification

While the preacher aims to bring unbelievers to a place of saving faith, the teacher aims to help believers to grow in understanding and obedience (sanctification). To be more specific, the teacher's objective is to coach believers in three key areas: in what to think, what to do and what to feel. These three areas correspond to the three aspects of the human soul – the mind, the will and the emotions. The teacher's main objective is to serve the church by describing right belief, right behaviour and right blessings. The teacher's vision is to equip people to believe the right things, to behave in the right way, and to experience the right, godly affections.

One of the best examples of this is the document known as the *Didache*, or 'The Teaching of the Twelve Apostles'. This is the oldest Christian document outside the New Testament and dates back to about the first century AD. It is composed of 16 chapters and it is effectively a manual of discipleship. It describes two ways of living: the path of life and the path of death. Its aim is clearly to instruct believers in how to live a truly Christian lifestyle. Just to take one example, chapter 2 section 2, about what to avoid:

You shall not kill; you shall not commit adultery; you shall not corrupt youth; you shall not commit fornication; you shall not steal; you shall not use soothsaying; you shall not practise sorcery; you shall not kill a child by abortion, neither shall you kill it when born; you shall not covet the goods of your neighbour . . .

Clearly, this is very practical teaching for those who have already become Christians. It shows once again the gift of teaching is the God-given ability to instruct *believers*.

Give me the book of God

The next part of the definition emphasises the content of teaching: the Bible. It is pretty clear from the writings of Paul that there were two principles on which he based his teaching. First, there was the Old Testament. As he puts it in 2 Timothy 3:16:

All Scripture is inspired by God and is useful to teach us what is true and to make us realize what is wrong in our lives. It straightens us out and teaches us to do what is right.

When Paul talks about 'Scripture' here, he is referring to the Hebrew Scriptures, or what we now call the Old Testament. Paul regarded these Scriptures as vital for 'teaching, rebuking, correcting and training in righteousness' (NIV).

The second main resource for Paul was the teaching of the Lord Jesus. For this reason, he says in Colossians 3:16: 'Let the words of Christ, in all their richness, live in your hearts and make you wise. Use his words to teach and counsel each other.'

Eventually, the writings of the Old Testament and the apostolic writings concerning Jesus were formed into one book that Christians simply know as 'the Bible'. It is this book, or rather collection of books, that forms the basis of our teaching today. True teachers are *Bible* teachers. They do not make Bible passages fit their thoughts. Rather, they allow Bible passages to dictate their thoughts. Teaching in the truest sense involves a clear exposition of what the Bible says in the power of the Holy Spirit. It is not based on human tradition or current theology but on the God-breathed book of God. The Bible is infallible because the God who inspired it, and the God whom it reveals, is infallible. It is truly the Maker's instructions.

One of the great challenges the teacher faces in today's postmodern culture has to do with the Bible's authority. Recently, a friend of mine in Christian leadership reported that there had been a split in his church. A man had started claiming that the Bible was no longer the ultimate authority for faith and life. In a short time, he had influenced a significant number of other people, and these had started to defy my friend's authority as the leader of the church. Within a short time, many had left.

This is not as uncommon as you might expect. There is such a disregard for authority generally today. So many people have grown up in dysfunctional, fatherless families. What authority they have known in their lives has been either unloving or rejecting. So they in turn reject everything that smacks of authority later on in life. One of the primary casualties of this is the Bible. The trouble is, once the authority of Scripture is questioned, the position of the teacher in a church is compromised too. As the stewards of the word of God, teachers lose their spiritual authority too.

I believe there is a desperate need today for teachers to help people rediscover the spiritual authority of the word of God. This can only be done if teachers fulfil their responsibility of making the Bible fresh and relevant to this generation. More than that, the Bible has to be taught in such a way that wounded people see the God revealed in Scripture as the one who can heal rather than exacerbate their wounds. It means speaking the truth in love, not teaching the Bible in a spirit of condemnation.

So do not neglect the word of God. True teaching is the God-given ability to instruct believers *in a biblical way*. The truly Spirit-filled person has a great regard and a deep hunger for the word of God. This is why, during seasons of revival, people have wept at the very sight of a Bible. Reading, studying and teaching the word is always restored to its rightful place in such seasons. The same Spirit who inspired the Bible now illuminates words and passages in the hearts of awakened believers. As John Wesley, the great evangelist of the eighteenth-century revival in England, exclaimed, 'O give me that book! At any price, give me the Book of God!'

There is a great picture of this kind of passion for the Bible in the book of Nehemiah chapter 8. The Temple had already been rebuilt under Zerubbabel in 516 BC. Now, half a century later, the city of Jerusalem has been restored. In celebration, Ezra brings out the Torah, the word of God. He stands on a platform to read. The whole nation stands in awe-struck silence, waiting with baited breath to hear the timeless words of God after a long and lamentable silence. Ezra praises God and the people bow down in worship. Then the Levites begin their ministry, instructing all the people who were standing in the square just inside the Water Gate. As Nehemiah reports: 'They read from the Book of the Law of God and clearly explained the meaning of what was being read, helping the people understand each passage' (Nehemiah 8:8). It is said that all the people wept as they heard the word of the Lord (v. 9).

What a great picture of a whole nation experiencing revival! And what a great reminder that in times of restoration the word of God becomes central once again. In seasons of awakening, people listen attentively to the reading of the word and are deeply moved by the power of its life-changing message. Men and women are raised up to instruct and teach in a way that affects the mind, emotions and will. How we need a renewal of this levitical ministry today. How we need the Father to raise up a generation of teachers who can instruct believers in a passionate way, and who are gifted at clearly explaining what the Bible says, helping the people to understand.

The revelation of the Holy Spirit

If it is vital to teach what the Bible says, it is also vital to teach in a prophetic way. It is not enough simply to repeat what the Bible says, let alone what other people have taught about the Bible. I remember my friend Dr R. T. Kendall saying how he had once read out the entire text of Jonathan Edwards' classic sermon, 'Sinners in the hands of an angry God'. In its own day, this message resulted in revival breaking out in an entire town in the USA. But 250 years later, R. T. Kendall's reading of it reduced his own congregation to a soporific stupor. While Edwards' message taught Bible truths, it was a word for his context and his day. Put another way, it was not just the hour for the message but the message for the hour.

When R. T. read it, the hour had well and truly passed long ago!

I believe the next most important factor for teachers, after being Bible-based, is being prophetic or Spirit-inspired. Teachers need the word of God, yes, but we also need the Spirit of God. We need the Scriptures, yes, but we also need God's power. It is for this reason that I conclude my definition of the gift of teaching with the word 'revelatory'. The gift of teaching is the God-given ability to instruct believers in a biblical and a *revelatory* way. Those who teach the Bible must not only transmit information, they must also communicate revelation. Information involves explaining the fixed meaning of a Bible passage. Revelation involves explaining the prophetic significance of the passage for today. Only when information is combined with revelation will we get transformation.

One of the best books on the art of Bible teaching is John Stott's *I Believe in Preaching*. He says:

> Without doubt the best sermons we ever preach to others are those we have first preached to ourselves. Or, to put the same truth somewhat differently, when God speaks to us through a text of Scripture, and it becomes luminous or phosphorescent to us, it is then that it continues to glow with divine glory when we seek to open it up to others.[3]

That is indeed true. The trouble is, nearly all the books on Bible teaching and preaching neglect to talk in any depth about the role of revelation in this process. Most books about 'preaching' are written by non-charismatics. While these have immense value, they ignore the dimension of

---

[3] John Stott, *I Believe in Preaching* (Hodder & Stoughton, 1988), p. 292.

the 'prophetic' in Bible teaching. They tend to be strong in the area of technical exposition, but weak in the area of prophetic application.

The primary reason for this is that most non-charismatics believe that the gift of prophecy died out with the apostles and that preaching has replaced prophecy. They reason thus: if prophecy in the New Testament involved declaring the mind of Christ to the church, this is no longer needed. Why? Because the Bible has now revealed everything we need to know about the mind of Christ. Teaching makes prophecy redundant.

The trouble is that this view simply cannot be sustained on the basis of what the Bible itself teaches. Paul consistently stresses that the two gifts of teaching and prophecy are different, and gives no indication whatsoever that the two would be fused at the dawn of the second century. Paul separates prophets and teachers in Ephesians 4:11 and he separates the gift of prophecy and the gift of teaching in Romans 12:6–7. The view that prophecy died out at the end of the first century, and that Bible teaching has now replaced prophecy, is not true to the writings of Paul or to the Bible as a whole. Paul envisaged that God's people would be exercising the gift of prophecy until 'the end comes' (1 Corinthians 13:10); that is, until the Second Coming. The same is also true of teaching.

How then do prophecy and teaching differ?

Prophecy is the God-given ability to receive and communicate what the Holy Spirit reveals in a given situation. You could say it is direct revelation consistent with the Bible. It is new revelation continuous with old revelation. It normally comes in the form of a vision, a picture, a dream, an impression and, very occasionally, in the audible voice of the Lord. It does not usually come in the form of a prepared message but rather in a spontaneous utterance. Its purpose is primarily exhortation, not instruction.[4]

Teaching, on the other hand, is the God-given ability to give fresh insights into the truth already revealed in Scripture. It is about giving new perspectives on old revelation. Indeed, the greatest evidence of the 'gift' of teaching is a person's ability to communicate fresh, Spirit-inspired insights into ancient Bible texts. It is the ability to surprise and delight people with both innovative interpretation and relevant application. It is that supernatural capacity to help people see something in the text that amazes them with its clarity, authority and relevance.

At this point, perhaps an example from my own experience might help to highlight the differences between these two gifts.

Recently, I went to speak at a conference. Before I went, I sensed the Holy Spirit leading me to certain scriptures and giving me insights from those passages. From Thursday morning until Sunday morning I attempted to communicate what I sensed the Lord had given to me. Opening up the Scriptures, I engaged in the task of teaching biblical truths in what I hoped was a revelatory way. In other words, I was exercising the gift of teaching.

On Sunday morning, however, I moved into a different gear. I had been troubled the previous three days by a growing sense that there was disunity in the church. People were praising God in song, but there was a disharmony at a relational level that was barely masked by the sound of music. It was just like it says in 1 Corinthians 13:1: 'If I could speak in any language in heaven or on earth but didn't love

---

[4] For more on the gift of prophecy, see Barry Kissell's *The Prophet's Notebook* (Kingsway, 2002).

others, I would only be making meaningless noise like a loud gong or a clanging cymbal.'

On the Sunday morning, the church leaders met to pray for the final meeting of the conference. My team and I joined them. As the people praised the Lord together, I remained seated, pondering in my heart the impressions that I felt the Spirit was giving me. As I did this, I became more and more troubled by the same sense of disunity. Unable to hold myself back any longer, I stood and spoke out what the Lord was laying on my heart. A spontaneous flow of words came out of my mouth, expressing the Father's heart cry for genuine and loving fellowship in the church. At the end, there was a shocked silence, and we all left for the main meeting.

As I sat waiting on the Lord during the opening songs, my interpreter came up to me and said, 'What you shared in the prayer meeting was a prophetic word from God. You need to share it with the whole congregation.' I hesitated because I had been asked to give a teaching on a Bible passage concerning revival. After a few moments' prayer, I decided I would ask the senior pastor of the church what he thought. He told me to deliver the same word that I had given in the prayer meeting, and so I climbed the platform and shared the word with the whole gathering.

What happened next was very moving. My interpreter started weeping, followed by the pastor and his wife, followed by the congregation. What I had not realised was that the local congregation had not accepted their new pastor and his wife, and that the previous pastor (much loved) was still worshipping there! That morning, scores of people rushed forward to ask forgiveness from the new pastor and his wife. It was thrilling to see the depth of the repentance and reconciliation taking place that day. For that, as always, all the glory goes to Jesus.

I tell this story not to paint myself in any great colours but simply to share out of my own experience the difference between prophecy and teaching. Up until Sunday, I was expounding Bible passages in what was (I trust) a revelatory way. That was teaching. What happened on the Sunday morning was different. I brought a spontaneous word of revelation consistent with the Scriptures. That, I believe, was prophecy. Prophecy and teaching are accordingly different gifts. They should not be confused.

At the same time, we need to remember the additional truth that every teacher has the gift of prophecy! All God's people can now prophesy, thanks to the outpouring of the Holy Spirit on the Day of Pentecost. This means that Bible teachers have the capacity to see visions and to dream dreams. They have the capacity to receive prophetic revelation as they prepare and deliver their teaching message. Although it is not true to say that all prophets can teach, it is true that all teachers can prophesy – at least once in a while!

The teacher must therefore resist the temptation to study and expound the Bible using the natural mind alone. If that happens, people merely receive academic lectures, and this does not feed them spiritually. Instead, the teacher needs to be constantly open to what the Holy Spirit is saying, both through the written word, and through direct 'words'. When the teacher begins to function in this more prophetic way, there is a rich and life-changing marriage of the word and the Spirit, the head and the heart, truth and experience, light and heat. The ancient, indeed timeless, words of the Bible suddenly seem as fresh as a new day as the Holy Spirit fixes his light on a word, a sentence or a passage. We begin to understand what Jonathan Edwards meant, when in the heights of a great awakening, he wrote:

> I had then, and at other times, the greatest delight in the Holy Scriptures. Oftentimes in reading it, every word seemed to touch my heart. I felt a harmony between something in my heart, and those sweet and powerful words. I seemed often to see so much light exhibited by every sentence, that I could not get along in reading; often dwelling long on one sentence, to see the wonders contained in it; and yet almost every sentence seemed to be full of wonders.

Are women permitted to teach?

A final question we cannot avoid is whether women are permitted to be Bible teachers. Some are adamant on the basis of 1 Timothy 2:11ff. that they are not. Others take a different view, on the basis of different Scripture passages, and argue that women are permitted to teach in the local church.

The discussion really revolves around Paul's instructions to Timothy concerning the role of women in 1 Timothy 2:11–15. Here is what Paul writes, in the New Living Translation:

> Women should listen and learn quietly and submissively. I do not let women teach men or have authority over them. Let them listen quietly. For God made Adam first, and afterward he made Eve. And it was the woman, not Adam, who was deceived by Satan, and sin was the result. But women will be saved through childbearing and by continuing to live in faith, love, holiness, and modesty.

Conservative evangelicals tend to argue that Paul plainly forbids women to teach in public worship meetings.

Furthermore, they contend that this is a universal principle, not a contingent one. In other words, this is a rule for all time, not just a rule for the local church to which Paul was writing. They appeal to Paul's comments about God creating Adam first, saying that this indicates something permanent.

While this is an understandable reading of the text, it is also open to question. Paul emphasises that it is he who forbids women to teach. 'I do not let women teach,' he writes. Readers need to decide carefully whether this personal ruling constitutes a divine and permanently binding principle.

How have Pentecostals and charismatics responded to the question 'Are women permitted to teach?' For the most part, they have responded more favourably. Though there are notable exceptions, most take the view that women can teach. They argue that the views expressed in 1 Timothy 2:11–15 are Paul's ruling for a particular situation, and that other Bible passages indicate that women can exercise the gift of teaching publicly.

Pentecostals and charismatic Bible scholars point to the account of the outpouring of the Spirit in Acts 2. On the Day of Pentecost, the result of the giving of the Spirit was that daughters as well as sons could now prophesy. As the NLT puts it, 'In those days I will pour out my Spirit upon all my servants, men and women alike, and they will prophesy' (Acts 2:18). The clear message of this passage is that women are supposed to operate in the gift of prophecy, as well as men. In the new democracy of the age of the Spirit, women can enjoy both the gift and the gifts of the Holy Spirit. Women are now able to prophesy, a word that in Luke's understanding clearly involves preaching.

If the reader is tempted to reply, 'But this is narrative, and it is Luke, not Paul,' then an appeal can be made to what Paul says in a letter. In Galatians 3:28 he writes: 'There is no longer Jew or Gentile, slave or free, male or female. For you are all Christians – you are one in Christ Jesus.' Paul is adamant that the dividing walls that fallen humanity erects are abolished in the body of Christ, the church. In essence, he is stressing what Luke says in Acts 2:13–18, that there is no room for racism, ageism, classism or sexism in the new age of the Spirit.

I personally warm to what Susan Hyatt says in her excellent article entitled 'Spirit-filled Women':

> At strategic times in salvation history, God has chosen women and empowered them with His Spirit to carry out His will in extraordinary ways. He chose Mary to give birth to the Saviour. He chose another Mary to be the first apostle to proclaim the Good News of His resurrection. And He chose women in the early church to pastor, teach, and proclaim the gospel. Women were co-workers with the apostle Paul and joint-heirs together with Christ and their brothers in the faith.

Susan Hyatt goes on to add, 'In the twentieth century, Spirit-filled women began to discover that these women were not exceptions to God's plan, but instead were His prototypes for God's woman.'[5]

You must decide for yourself whether this truly reflects the will of God.

---

[5] Susan Hyatt, 'Spirit-filled Women', in Vinson Synan *The Century of the Holy Spirit* (Thomas Nelson, 2001), p. 262.

In conclusion

The gift of teaching is the God-given ability to instruct believers in a biblical and a revelatory way.

On the one hand, every believer has the ability to study the word of God and to share their insights with other believers; that is, every believer has the capacity to teach other believers in an informal, rudimentary way. This is clear from Colossians 3:16, where Paul talks about letting the words of Jesus dwell in our hearts so that we can be wise and teach and counsel each other.

On the other hand, certain believers grow and excel in this ability so much that they are recognised as having a charisma or grace-gift of teaching. If they prove faithful in the low-profile use of this gift, they may well find themselves released to exercise it with greater visibility. This, I believe, can apply to both men and women. This will usually lead to a governmental expression of the gift and will involve being a part of the leadership of a local church. When that happens, the person in question has entered into the ministry of the teacher (Ephesians 4:11).

From all this, we can see the importance of the teacher in the church today. Though the teacher may be mentioned last in the list in Ephesians 4:11, this does not imply least in importance. All five ministries are essential for a healthy church. As Paul goes on to say in Ephesians 4:12–14:

> Their responsibility is to equip God's people to do his work and build up the church, the body of Christ, until we come to such unity in our faith and knowledge of God's Son that we will be mature and full grown in the Lord, measuring up to the full stature of Christ. Then we will no longer be like children, forever changing our minds about what we believe . . .

Apostles, prophets, evangelists, pastors and teachers are *all* vital if churches are to grow, and Paul gives four reasons why.

The first reason is to 'equip' believers to do God's work. The five ministries – including that of the teacher – enable believers to do the work of the church (which is not always the same as church work). This is in fact what I admired most about John Wimber. He was a man who had an extraordinary ability to equip others. His teaching was always Bible-based and very practical. He made hard things simple and released others to do what they saw him doing. He was truly a coach.

The second reason is to 'build' believers. Paul says that believers are to be prepared or equipped 'so that the body of Christ may be built up'. The teaching gift is a building gift. As Paul warns, 'each one should be careful how he builds' (NIV). We are called to build on the foundation of Jesus and to build that which will survive testing by fire (1 Corinthians 3:10–15). For this we need God's wisdom, not our own. As it says in Proverbs 24:3–4: 'A house is built by wisdom and becomes strong through good sense. Through knowledge its rooms are filled with all sorts of precious riches and valuables.'

The third reason is to 'mature' believers. The five gifts are given so that believers become mature, attaining to the whole measure of the stature of Christ. Teachers play an essential part in helping believers to grow up. While Christians are called to be 'childlike', they are not supposed to be 'childish'. Good teaching helps to create an environment where we are no longer infants in the faith (Ephesians 4:14; see also Colossians 1:28).

The fourth reason is to 'stabilise' believers. This is perhaps a rather strange word, but the writer says that

teachers help to prevent believers from being tossed back
and forth by the waves and winds of deception. This naut-
ical picture is particularly helpful when we look at the
teaching ministry. Good teachers help to create stability
when the storm clouds threaten. In the case of a seafaring
yacht, what lies beneath the surface is more important
than what is above. If what is below is not heavier than
what is above, then the vessel will sink. A church is like
an ocean-going vessel. Unless there is substance and
depth to it, it will very likely capsize. Teachers help to
create the strong keel that enables believers to negotiate
the storms of life.

That being the case, no church can afford to be without
at least one person with the God-given ability to instruct
believers in a biblical and a revelatory way. Like apostles,
prophets, evangelists and pastors, the Bible teacher has a
crucial role in the body of Christ, equipping, building,
maturing and stabilising believers. All five of these leadership ministries are crucial for church health and church
growth.

QUESTION TIME

- Do you have an ability to teach others?
- Is this ability a spiritual gift?
- Is this gift recognised by others?
- Are you Bible-based in what you teach?
- Do you revere and study the word of God?
- Are you able to explain the meaning of passages clearly and accurately?
- Do you exercise the gift of prophecy?
- Are you growing in the prophetic?
- When you teach from the Bible, do you apply it prophetically?
- Does your teaching equip others?
- Does it build rather than tear down the church?
- Does it help believers to grow in maturity?
- Does it stabilise the church and protect it against deception?

2

Learning from Jesus

There are, it is said, three types of teacher. There are those you listen to, those you can't listen to, and those you can't help listening to. Jesus was the third kind.

One of the surest facts about Jesus was that he had a unique and marvellous ministry of teaching. Even the learned theologian Nicodemus admitted as much when he said, 'Rabbi, we know you are a teacher who has come from God. For no-one could perform the miraculous signs you are doing if God were not with him' (John 3:2, NIV). Just about everyone addressed Jesus as 'Teacher'. His disciples used this form of address (e.g. Mark 4:38), as did unnamed individuals (Mark 9:17; 10:17), the Pharisees (Matthew 9:11), members of synagogues (Mark 5:35), the Herodians (Matthew 22:16), the Sadducees (Matthew 22:24), tax collectors (Matthew 17:24), and the scribes (Matthew 8:19).

Everywhere Jesus went he taught people. This ministry was not confined to the synagogues, though he frequently taught there (e.g. Luke 4:15). Jesus also taught in people's homes (Mark 2:1–2), in the countryside (Matthew 5:1–2), in towns and cities (Matthew 11:1), and in the Temple

(Matthew 26:55). On at least one occasion he even taught from a boat (Luke 5:2). In fact, one of the charges against Jesus at his trial was this: 'He stirs up the people all over Judea by his teaching. He started in Galilee and has come all the way here' (Luke 23:5, NIV). Clearly, Jesus taught openly and his ministry had a massive impact on many people.

There is a Japanese proverb that states: 'Better than a thousand days of diligent study is one day with a great teacher.' If we could wind back the clock and roll back the years, what would we learn from a day spent with the greatest teacher that ever lived? What would we notice about the content and the method of his teaching?

Revelatory in its content

I think the first thing we would notice is that Jesus' teaching was full of divine revelation. Listening to Jesus, and indeed watching him, we would quickly see that he did not consult other rabbis or learned books but he consulted his Father in heaven. His teaching arose out of times of intimate communion with his Father. His private and public teaching was the result of listening to the voice of God.

The keynote of Jesus' entire teaching ministry can be found in his words recorded in John 12:49–50:

> For I did not speak of my own accord, but the Father who sent me commanded me what to say and how to say it. I know that his command leads to eternal life. So whatever I say is just what the Father has told me to say. (NIV)

For me, this is the clue to Jesus' effectiveness as a teacher. In his affectionate relationship with the Father, Jesus heard everything that he needed to communicate to others. When he was with the crowds on the mountain, Jesus heard the Father telling him what to say and how to say it (Matthew 5:1ff.). When confronted by the Pharisees, Jesus again heard the Father telling him the content and the form of what to say (Matthew 12:22ff.). The same is true when Jesus was on his own with the disciples (Matthew 24:1ff.).

It follows from this that the highest priority for a teacher today is intimacy with the Father. The deeper the teacher's devotional life, the deeper the teaching will be. We have the awesome privilege of being adopted as sons and daughters of the Father of creation. We can spend time with him every day, holding his hand, listening to his tender voice. Those entrusted with the ministry of teaching need to spend time in childlike openness to the father heart of God. Our God is a great and holy God, but he is also an extremely kind father, who is always eager to share his thoughts with us.

I like the story of a man who owned a chain of supermarkets. He was an extremely influential and powerful man. One day, he took his five-year-old son with him on his 'rounds' of the shops. The little boy looked on him in awe and wonder as his dad related to his staff and they to him, their boss. After visiting four or five big shops, they returned to the car. The little boy said, thoughtfully, 'Daddy, do all these people know that you can talk like Donald Duck?'

During his earthly ministry, Jesus enjoyed unbroken communion with the Father who made the heavens and the earth. This was the secret wellspring of the revelatory teaching that he gave. If this was true for the Son of God, how much more is it true for God's adopted children?

We need to invest in ever-increasing intimacy with the Father if we are to hear his voice and communicate his life-changing truth. Jesus spent a significant part of his ministry on his own, listening to the Father. Luke reports that Jesus often withdrew to the wilderness to pray (Luke 5:16). In the very next verse he says: 'One day while Jesus was teaching . . .' (Luke 5:17). We cannot speak in the public place unless we have first listened in the private place.

Anointed by the Spirit

I think the second thing we would notice, if we spent 24 hours with Jesus, is the anointing on his life and teaching. We need constantly to remember that Jesus did not start teaching publicly until he had been baptised in the River Jordan by John. When that happened, the Holy Spirit came down upon Jesus like a dove and the Father spoke words of affirmation and endearment. From that moment on, for a period of about three years, Jesus travelled principally in Galilee and Judea teaching people. The anointing given to Jesus at his baptism was the power behind his preaching.

Jesus himself acknowledged that his teaching ministry was the result of the anointing of the Holy Spirit. In his very first sermon, he quoted the prophet Isaiah, saying: 'The Spirit of the Lord is on me, because he has anointed me to preach good news to the poor' (Luke 4:18, NIV). This once and for all proves that Jesus' teaching was not the result of his natural ability but of the Holy Spirit's anointing. In Chapter 1, I defined the gift of teaching as 'the God-given ability to instruct believers in a biblical and a revelatory way'. Jesus was given this supernatural ability from the moment of his baptism onwards.

What was the evidence of this supernatural anointing? The first evidence was the authority of Jesus' words. Just about everyone remarked on the authority of Jesus' teaching. In Mark 1:21–22 we read:

> Jesus and his companions went to the town of Capernaum, and every Sabbath day he went into the synagogue and taught the people. They were amazed at his teaching, for he taught as one who had real authority – quite unlike the teachers of religious law.

At the end of that same episode, we learn that the people were all so amazed that they asked each other: 'What sort of new teaching is this? . . . It has such authority!' (Mark 1:27).

What is the point being made here? Simply this. In Jesus' day the scribes were the teachers of the Law. These men taught by quoting well-known rabbis. They tried to acquire spiritual authority through quoting other influential teachers. In other words, the authority of their teaching was derived from the scholars of the past and the present. It came by association with the views of erudite teachers.

Jesus, on the other hand, was entirely different. Unlike the scribes, he did not go around quoting celebrated religious gurus. His authority was direct, not derived. It came straight from God Almighty, the highest authority in the universe. Furthermore, unlike the scribes, Jesus did not regurgitate the old views of various religious schools and traditions. Rather, he taught about the kingdom of God. He communicated the fact that the dynamic reign of

God had arrived. In short, he taught a *now* word and he taught a *new* word. He was less interested in what people had said yesterday, and was more interested in what God was saying today. He was less interested in repeating old traditions and more interested in the new revelation given to him by the Father. It is for this reason that we often find a response of amazement in Jesus' listeners: 'After Jesus finished speaking, the crowds were amazed at his teaching, for he taught as one who had real authority – quite unlike the teachers of religious law' (Matthew 7:28–29).

It might be asked to what degree this aspect of Jesus' example can be a model for today's Bible teacher. If Jesus brings a new word, does that mean the teacher brings a new word too? It is important to remember what I said in Chapter 1. Today's Bible teacher brings a new insight into an old word (that is, the Bible). But the teacher does not add new content to the New Covenant teaching of Jesus.

The second indication of the anointing is the power of his works. Jesus did not communicate with words alone. He also taught by works. On the one hand, Jesus *proclaimed* that God's reign had arrived on the earth. On the other hand, he actually *proved* this claim by setting people free from their sicknesses and oppression. Since we will devote much of the next chapter to this subject, I will restrict myself to this one comment: anyone who exercises the gift of teaching today needs to keep praying for more and more of the Spirit's anointing. With the anointing of the Spirit, teaching is a rich combination of message and miracles:

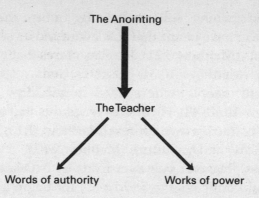

Biblical in its source

The third thing I think we would notice about Jesus is the fact that his teaching was rooted in the written word of God. Jesus did not come to pass on human traditions but to expound afresh the word of God. Jesus clearly revered the Hebrew Scriptures. As he himself said in Matthew 5:17–18:

> Don't misunderstand why I have come. I did not come to abolish the law of Moses or the writings of the prophets. No, I came to fulfil them. I assure you, until heaven and earth disappear, even the smallest detail of God's law will remain until its purpose is achieved.

Right from the beginning of his teaching ministry, Jesus relies on the written word of God. Indeed, we should remember that the first thing that happens after his baptism is the temptation of Jesus in the desert. Jesus successfully resists the devil by quoting three passages of Old Testament Scripture (Matthew 4:1–11). Jesus makes his stand with the authority of Scripture: 'For the Scriptures say . . .' he declares.

In his teaching, Jesus constantly quotes the Hebrew Bible. 'You have heard that the law of Moses says . . .' he proclaims (Matthew 5:21). He cites verses that explain his mission (Matthew 10:34; 13:13–15) and refers to Old Testament people whose lives foreshadow his own (Matthew 12:40–42). He quotes scriptures that speak prophetically into his own context (Matthew 11:10, 17; 15:8–9; 21:16; 26:31) and the future (Matthew 24:29). He asks the Pharisees, 'Haven't you ever read . . . ?' (Matthew 12:3; 21:42) and criticises the Sadducees for being ignorant of the Scriptures (Matthew 22:29).

Jesus' teaching was based on God's word, not human perspectives. As Jesus said to the Pharisees, 'by your own tradition, you nullify the direct commandment of God' (Matthew 15:6). When Jesus was challenged about an issue of ethics, he did not toe a party line but he reminded his listeners what the Bible said, even when that involved saying something tough (as in his teaching on divorce in Matthew 19:1–12). When Jesus was challenged about an issue of faith, again he relied totally on what the Bible says (as in his teaching on the Messiah's authority in Matthew 22:41–46). In all matters of belief and behaviour, the Bible was the basis for Jesus' teaching. Even when Jesus was dying on the cross, he was still quoting the Scriptures (Matthew 27:46), and he did not stop once he had been raised (Luke 24:27).

Those who teach in the church should expound what the Bible says. Speaking personally, when I hear a sermon, I do not primarily want to hear the preacher's views, let alone the views of some religious tradition or report. First and foremost, I want to hear a Christ-like explanation of what God has said in his eternal word. I want to listen to a person who communicates biblical and kingdom truths in a relevant and revelatory way. That is what Jesus did. That is what we should do, too.

Relevant to its listeners

The next thing I think we would notice about Jesus' teaching would be its relevance. Look at some of the topics Jesus speaks about. These are just some of the selected highlights from Matthew's Gospel: anger (Matthew 5:21–26), sex (5:27–30), divorce (5:31–32), swearing (5:33–37), revenge (5:38–47), giving (6:1–4), prayer (6:5–15), fasting (6:16–18), money (6:19–24), anxiety (6:25–34), judging others (7:1–6), hygiene (15:1–20).

Jesus taught about what the people needed to hear, rather than what they wanted to hear. His teaching was extremely relevant to the whole of their lives. His focus was on helping people to live the lifestyle of the kingdom of God. In other words, he communicated principles that would enable his listeners to place everything under the dynamic rule of Almighty God. While he taught about spiritual disciplines like giving, prayer and fasting, he did not restrict himself to talking about religious practices. Rather, he instructed his listeners about all facets of life: their moods, their possessions, their relationships, their work, their speech, and so on.

As teachers, we need to have a good understanding of the issues that face believers today. Many if not all of the issues Jesus taught about are still pertinent today. It would be an interesting exercise to take the summary of topics listed above and ask when you last heard a sermon on one of these subjects – or when you last gave one, for that matter! Most people come to church today with hurts, habits and hang-ups. Do we know our people well enough to be able to identify how they are feeling? Do we know how to communicate in a relevant way on these issues? Do we know the needs of our flock?

Recently, some research was conducted on the relevance of preaching in today's churches. Using a wide range of respondents, the researcher tried to discover the level of relevance in the preaching in their local church. The results were very revealing. While many of the respondents found their minister's preaching 'helpful', most found it 'irrelevant'. In fact, 84 per cent of those polled chose to respond on the issue of relevance, and out of that number 47 per cent said that the preaching was marked by a lack of relevance.

The results of this questionnaire are interesting. They reveal that while preaching today is often spiritually uplifting, it is also irrelevant for many of the people who attend. Many people given the task of teaching believers are simply not following the example of Jesus and communicating biblical, kingdom principles for the family, the workplace, the community, and so on. This lack of connection with the ordinary lives of ordinary people is something all of us need to address. People today are crying out for the kind of integrated spirituality modelled by Jesus. They want to know how to be like Jesus on Monday morning at their workplace, not just Sunday morning in the worship place. They want to be practical, rather than pious.

Given that we have two ears and only one mouth, those of us who teach should be twice at good at listening as we are at speaking. Jesus listened to what others were thinking and saying. In Luke 5:21–22 we see the following exchange:

'Who does this man think he is?' the Pharisees and teachers of religious law said to each other. 'This is blasphemy! Who but God can forgive sins?' Jesus knew what they were thinking, so he asked them, 'Why do you think this is blasphemy?'

We should underline these words: 'Jesus knew what they were thinking'. Do we know what people are thinking as we teach them? Are we aware of the issues that worry, wound and weary them? Or do we just carry on with what we want to say?

So, how do we know what people are thinking?

The first way is to ask God. You can ask the Father for revelation by his Holy Spirit. As you prepare and deliver your message, you can ask the Lord to give you the gifts of prophecy and discernment to help you know what is really going on in the hearts of the people.

The second is to ask the people. You can spend time visiting, talking, telephoning and emailing, in order to connect with the real issues that are going on in their lives. In other words, you can choose to dialogue with your listeners. Like Jesus, you can employ a *relational* model of teaching. Relevance is directly related to relationship. The relevance of the teaching is proportionate to the relational life of the teacher. Perhaps this is why pastors and teachers are found so close together in the list of the five ministries in Ephesians 4:11. Every teacher needs a pastoral heart.

It has been said of Jonathan Edwards, the great eighteenth-century theologian of revival, that his knowledge of the Bible, evidenced in his sermons, is probably unrivalled. But it is also said that his knowledge of the human heart, and its operations, has scarcely been equalled.

Do we know the hearts of the people we are teaching?

One influential Christian leader's son was asked why he no longer went to church. He replied, 'I gave up on church because that man the preacher was saying all the right things, in all the right language, but he wasn't saying it to anyone. He didn't know who I was or where I was, and it would never occur to him to ask.'

We need to have the humility to ask the people in our churches what their real needs are. We need to present Jesus in a way that is relevant for *everyone*.

THE MANY NAMES OF CHRIST

To the artist, He is the One Altogether Lovely.
To the architect, He is the Chief Cornerstone.
To the baker, He is the Living Bread.
To the banker, He is the Hidden Treasure.
To the biologist, He is the Life.
To the builder, He is the Sure Foundation.
To the carpenter, He is the Door.
To the doctor, He is the Great Physician.
To the educator, He is the Great Teacher.
To the farmer, He is the Sower and Lord of the Harvest.
To the florist, He is the Lily of the Valley and the Rose of
    Sharon.
To the geologist, He is the Rock of Ages.
To the horticulturist, He is the True Vine.
To the jeweller, He is the Pearl of Great Price.
To the juror, He is the True Witness.
To the lawyer, He is the Righteous Judge.
To the oculist, He is the Light of the Eyes.
To the philosopher, He is the Wisdom of God.
To the servant, He is the Good Master.
To the student, He is the Incarnate Truth.

To the theologian, He is the Author and Finisher of our
   faith.
To the toiler, He is the Giver of Rest.
To the sinner, He is the Lamb of God that takes away the sin
   of the world.
To the Christian, He is the Son of the Living God, the
   Saviour, the Redeemer and Lord!

(author unknown)

Compassionate in its motivation

The next thing that I believe we would notice about Jesus'
teaching is its compassion. Compassion literally means
'suffering with someone'. It means coming alongside
those in need and empathising with their lives. This is
exactly what Jesus did. He was born as a human being
and humbled himself, living as a servant of all. He identified with sinful, wounded human beings and, as a
result, was able to teach into their lives with pertinence
and integrity. He did not walk among people as one aloof
from the joys and sorrows of human life. Rather, he lived
a truly incarnate life, experiencing the triumphs and the
trials of this world. The driving force for his teaching ministry was compassion. As it says in Mark 6:34: 'A vast
crowd was there as he stepped from the boat, and he
had compassion on them because they were like sheep
without a shepherd. So he taught them many things.'

People do not care how much you know until they
know how much you care. I believe one of the most
compelling things about Jesus' teaching ministry was his
compassionate love.

I once heard a story about a missionary called Father
Damien. In 1873, this Catholic priest heard a call from
God to go and minister to a colony of 700 lepers on the

island of Molokai. He was there for over ten years, ministering the Father's love without much breakthrough. Then, one morning in 1885, he got up and made himself a cup of tea. Accidentally, he spilled the boiling water from the kettle on his toes. Out of instinct he winced, but in reality he felt no pain at all. There was no feeling in his foot. The following Sunday, he looked out at his congregation and began, 'We lepers . . .'

Jesus did not treat others like containers into which one pours information. He treated others as human beings, and taught them out of compassionate love rather than proud detachment. To quote the prophet Isaiah, Jesus taught as 'a man of sorrows, and familiar with suffering' (Isaiah 53:3, NIV). Jesus did not teach using a 'jug to mug' approach, but rather a 'heart to heart' methodology. We need to do the same. We need to learn to speak words of grace. At the end of his first sermon, it was said, 'All who were there spoke well of him and were amazed by the gracious words that fell from his lips. "How can this be?" they asked. "Isn't this Joseph's son?"' (Luke 4:22). 'The Lord is compassionate and gracious', says the psalmist (Psalm 103:8, NIV). Does our teaching exhibit these qualities?

No one can deny that there was tremendous skill in Jesus' teaching. But of greater importance was the great love that motivated it. As John Ruskin once put it, 'When love and skill work together, expect a masterpiece.'

No wonder Jesus painted so many verbal masterpieces.

Visual in its appeal

Jesus was a master at capturing people's attention and he did so through the use of apt analogies and provocative parables. All of these are what are known as 'invitational' forms of speech. Jesus was simply the best when it came to this kind of language. No wonder he attracted big crowds. As it says in Mark 12:37 (NIV), 'The large crowd listened to him with delight.' The word translated 'delight' is *hedeos* in the Greek. It means 'sweetly', 'gladly', or 'with pleasure'. The best teachers and preachers are those who delight as well as instruct.

Martin Luther once said: 'People are captivated more readily by comparisons and examples than by difficult and subtle disputations. They would rather see a well-drawn picture than a well-written book.'

Jesus provided well-drawn pictures in his teaching. The usual method was to paint a word-picture through an analogy or a parable. This was an accepted way of teaching in the Jewish culture of Jesus' day. Rabbis would ask their pupils: *lemah hadaver domeh*, meaning, 'To what can this be compared?' Or they would say: *enshol lekha mashal*, 'Let me tell you a parable.' Jesus taught using analogies. He asked, 'How can I describe the Kingdom of God? What story should I use to illustrate it?' (Mark 4:30). He also taught using parables. A parable is simply the elaboration of an analogy into a story: 'He used many such stories and illustrations to teach the people as much as they were able to understand. In fact, in his public teaching he taught only with parables . . .' (Mark 4:33–34).

Jesus used features of everyday life to illustrate kingdom principles. In Matthew's Gospel alone, we find

the following: salt (Matthew 5:13), light (5:14–16), gates
(7:13–14), roads (7:14), trees (7:15–20), houses (7:24–27),
foxes and birds (8:20), brides and bridegrooms (9:15),
wine (9:16–17), farmers (13:1–9), weeds (13:24–30), seeds
(13:31–32), bread (13:33), treasure (13:44–46), fishing
(13:47–49), plants (15:13), pits (15:14), dogs (15:26),
weather (16:1–4), rocks (16:18), mountains (17:20), sheep
(18:10–14), vineyards (20:1–16), lamps (25:1–3).

At other times, he used a physical object rather than a
verbal picture. When questioned by the Pharisees about
paying taxes, Jesus' response was to show them a Roman
coin (Matthew 22:15–22).

'Here, show me the Roman coin used for the tax.' When they
handed him the coin, he asked, 'Whose picture and title are
stamped on it?' 'Caesar's,' they replied. 'Well, then,' he said,
'give to Caesar what belongs to him. But everything that
belongs to God must be given to God.'

When Jesus entered into a conversation with a woman at
a well, he used the water in the well as the primary visual
aid for what he wanted to teach (John 4:4–42). When Jesus
talked about the coming of the kingdom of God, he
pointed to a fig tree (Matthew 24:32–33).

Jesus made his teaching more accessible and memorable through the rich use of illustrations. One of the most
appealing things about Jesus' teaching is that he made
profound things very simple. In fact, he made them so
simple that children as well as adults could understand
them. This, I suggest, is the mark of a great teacher.

So a good teacher uses good illustrations. These can be
visual aids like coins, or water, or figs. Or they can be apt
analogies or striking stories. An effective communicator

knows when an illustration is needed to maintain the short attention span of people today. More than that, the effective communicator knows exactly what kind of illustration will best illuminate the biblical, kingdom principle in question. The great virtue of illustrations is that they communicate affectively, not just cognitively. They touch the heart in order to tease the mind.

Varied in its approach

I think the next thing we would notice about Jesus' teaching would be its variety. Jesus used parables, but he used other speech forms as well. For example, he used puns. Perhaps the most famous is in John 3:8, where Jesus uses a word that can mean both 'Spirit' (as in Holy Spirit) and 'wind'. This play on words creates two levels of meaning, the spiritual and the literal. The key is to get beyond the literal and see the spiritual.

Jesus also used questions. So, for example, in Mark 2:9, Jesus asks his listeners, 'Is it easier to say to the paralysed man, "Your sins are forgiven" or "Get up, pick up your mat, and walk"?'

How often do you pose questions to your congregation when you are teaching? We should remember the old proverb that true teaching is not a matter of filling a bucket but of lighting a fire. By asking a provocative question, we can help to ignite a holy curiosity in someone's heart.

Jesus also used proverbs. These are words of wisdom expressing profound truths in a simple and pithy way. Jesus frequently used terse sayings to express kingdom truths. He said, 'It is easier for a camel to go through the eye of a needle than for a rich person to enter the

Kingdom of God!' (Matthew 19:24). Proverbial sayings are a great resource for any teacher: 'When the devil reminds you of your past, you remind him of his future'; 'Jesus came not only to comfort the afflicted but to afflict the comfortable'. Good teachers use words of wisdom to maximum and memorable effect.

Jesus also used paradoxes. In fact, a lot of Jesus' teaching revels in apparent contradictions: 'Humble people get exalted'; 'Trying to save your life will result in you losing it'; 'Persecuted people are happy people'. Paradox is a great weapon in the teacher's armoury. If you are looking for a few kingdom contradictions, try these on for size:

A TRUE BELIEVER IS . . .

Strong enough to be weak
Successful enough to fail
Wise enough to say, 'I don't know'
Serious enough to laugh
Rich enough to be poor
Right enough to say 'I'm wrong'
Mature enough to be childlike
Planned enough to be spontaneous
Controlled enough to be flexible
Free enough to endure captivity
Knowledgeable enough to ask questions
Loving enough to be angry
Great enough to be anonymous
Responsible enough to play
Assured enough to be rejected
Stable enough to cry
Victorious enough to lose.

So there is considerable variety in Jesus' teaching method. Alongside analogies and parables, he used puns, questions, proverbs and paradoxes. At other times, he used hyperbole (exaggeration), irony, poetry and riddles. What all these things have in common is brevity and economy. Jesus did sometimes preach at length (Mark 6:34; Matthew 5–7). But a lot of the time his message was short, settling a matter with a great one-liner. Now this is extremely challenging to most of us. Often we can go on too long as teachers. We can take 45 minutes to say something that could be said a lot more succinctly. In much preaching, when all is said and done, a lot has been said and very little done.

If you are prone to this particular failing, then remember President William Harrison. In 1841, he gave the longest presidential inaugural address ever – running on for nearly two hours. It took place during a snowstorm, during which Harrison was wearing neither a hat nor a coat. He died of pneumonia a month later. There has to be a lesson in that somewhere.

Practical in its application

I think the next thing we might notice about Jesus' teaching is how practical it was. Jesus taught by 'doing'. He practised what he preached, and he got others to practise it too.

Much of Jesus' teaching is by example. Luke 11.1 is very revealing: 'Once when Jesus had been out praying, one of his disciples came to him as he finished and said, "Lord, teach us to pray, just as John taught his disciples."' It was Jesus actually praying that stimulated his disciples to want to pray. Similarly, it was Jesus demonstrating how to heal the sick and cast out demons that encouraged the disciples to learn how to do it themselves. Jesus taught by example. He walked the talk. Sometimes, his actions themselves were a sermon. So, for example, sitting and eating with tax collectors and sinners was a message in itself. It said something vital about the Messiah and it said something wonderful about the kingdom of God. This shows the importance of teaching by demonstration and not just by information. Those of us who teach must constantly remember the power of our example. We can preach a far better sermon with our lives than with our lips. As Jesus said, 'The student shares the teacher's fate. The servant shares the master's fate' (Matthew 10:25).

At the same time, Jesus asked others to respond practically to his words. So, for example, in Matthew's Gospel, Jesus says:

- 'Come, follow me' (Matthew 4:19, NIV)
- 'Go, show yourself to the priest' (Matthew 8:4, NIV)
- 'Get up, take your mat, and go home' (Matthew 9:6, NIV)
- 'Go, preach this message' (Matthew 10:7, NIV)
- 'Go to the lake and throw out your line' (Matthew 17:27, NIV)
- 'Go, sell your possessions' (Matthew 19:21, NIV)
- 'Go and tell my brothers' (Matthew 28:10, NIV)
- 'Go and make disciples' (Matthew 28:19, NIV)

Jesus did not expect others simply to sit and listen. Put another way, Jesus believed in 'active' rather than 'passive' learning. The disciples learnt by hearing, by seeing and by doing. This is one of the big reasons why they were able to continue the work of Jesus after his death. As the Chinese proverb says, 'Give a person a fish and you will feed them for a day. Teach them to fish and you feed them for a lifetime.'

As teachers, we need to equip and release others to go and do what we have taught in their own lives. We learn and remember:

- 10 per cent of what we hear
- 15 per cent of what we see
- 20 per cent of what we see and hear
- 40 per cent of what we discuss with others
- 80 per cent of what we experience directly

This is essential to effective teaching. We need to help people to learn by doing, not just by hearing.

Fearless in its delivery

One last thing we would no doubt notice about Jesus the teacher was his bravery. He was utterly fearless as he spoke to the disciples, the crowds and especially to his enemies. Secure as he was in the Father's love for him, he was able to teach from the firm foundation of faith, rather than the shaky foundation of fear.

One of the most extraordinary moments in the Gospels comes just before Jesus' passion, when the Pharisees and Herodians try to trap Jesus on the matter of paying taxes to Caesar. This is how they preface their question: 'Teacher, we know how honest you are. You teach about the way of God regardless of the consequences. You are impartial and don't have favourites' (Matthew 22:16). What an amazing statement! Even Jesus' enemies acknowledged that he practised what he preached and that he taught God's way truthfully. More than that, they correctly stated that Jesus was not affected by a fear of man in his teaching ministry. He was a God-pleaser rather than a man-pleaser.

The thing that I find perverse here is that Jesus' enemies should accept that he was a genuine teacher and yet reject his teaching. It was President Theodore Roosevelt who said, 'One of the great marvels of creation is the infinite capacity of the human brain to withstand the introduction of knowledge.' This is precisely what the Pharisees and the Herodians are doing here. They are withstanding the introduction of kingdom knowledge from the lips of Jesus. And yet (assuming they are not being sarcastic) they accept that he is a teacher who has 'integrity' (NIV)! Or, literally, a teacher who has 'truth'.

Jesus had to deal with perverse people a lot of the time in his teaching ministry. The worrying thing is that the most frequent examples of this are among the religious people (like the Pharisees) rather than the general public. Yet the noticeable thing about Jesus is that he does not cower under the pressure of criticism, nor does he falter under the weight of peer pressure, but rather he lives to say only what the Father is saying. What matters to him is that he pleases the Father, not those around him.

Here we return to the very first quality of Jesus' teaching mentioned in this chapter: dependence on the Father. In John 8:28–29, Jesus gives us the clue to his courage: 'I do nothing on my own, but I speak what the Father taught me. And the one who sent me is with me – he has not deserted me. For I always do those things that are pleasing to him.'

Highlight those words, 'I always do those things that are pleasing to him'. Herein is the source of Jesus' fearless teaching ministry. It is because Jesus lives to please his Father that his Father is always with him. It is because his Father is always with him that Jesus speaks out what the Father is teaching him. The secret is to stand before a congregation and to say to yourself, 'What these people think of me doesn't matter. I am here to please you, Father. I thank you that I am secure in the knowledge of your love. I rest in that revelation, and from this place of intimacy I will speak out what you want taught to these people at this particular time.'

Does this mean that the Bible teacher will never be tentative? If the issue at stake is our security in God, then we should not be tentative. If the issue at stake is one of truth, then where the teaching of Scripture is plain and clear, again we should not be timid or diffident. However, whenever we are called to speak on an issue of complexity and sensitivity, then humility and honesty are called for. There have been times when I have tackled a particularly difficult subject and I've had to admit that and be open with the congregation about it.

The greatest teacher

At the beginning of this chapter, I quoted a Japanese proverb: 'Better than a thousand days of diligent study is one day with a great teacher.' In this chapter we have spent a day with the greatest teacher of all time.

It has been said that Socrates and Aristotle each taught for 40 years, Plato for 50 years, but Jesus for only three. Yet his influence far surpasses the combined 130 years of teaching by these men who are acknowledged as the greatest philosophers of all antiquity. He painted no pictures, yet the finest paintings of Raphael, Michelangelo and Leonardo da Vinci received their illumination from him. He wrote no poetry, yet Dante, Milton and others of the world's greatest poets were inspired by him. He composed no music, yet Haydn, Handel, Beethoven and Bach reached their highest perfection in hymns, symphonies and oratorios composed in his honour. Jesus is quite simply the greatest teacher who ever lived.

In this chapter, we have identified some of the qualities that demonstrate the greatness of Jesus' teaching. You might join me in making these a kind of check-list for your own ministry. You might find it helpful to review each message you give in the light of the characteristics described here.

Our chief aim and our great desire must be to be like Jesus. There can be no greater example or inspiration than him. Those of us called to the ministry of teaching need constantly to be looking to Jesus. There are many models of teaching in the world and the church today. But we cannot go far wrong if we use Jesus as the Way.

As Abraham Lincoln once said, 'No one ever got lost walking on a straight road.'

QUESTION TIME

The teacher's check-list

Jesus' teaching	*My teaching*
Revelatory	Did my last message arise out of revelation from the Father?
Anointed	What evidence of the anointing was there?
Biblical	Were my thoughts based upon what the Bible says?
Relevant	Did I connect with the people?
Compassionate	Was I loving?
Visual	Did I use stories and pictures that had impact?
Varied	Did I vary my method?
Practical	Did I teach what I am living? And did it encourage a response?
Fearless	Did I faithfully and obediently communicate the truth?

3

Ministering with Power

When I am coaching other Bible teachers, I encourage them to communicate with fire. I use the word *fire* as an acrostic. It stands for:

F = Faithful to the Scriptures
I = Inspired by the Spirit
R = Relevant to the audience
E = Enthusiastic in the delivery

In Chapter 4 we will be looking at the first of these four priorities, being 'faithful to the Scriptures'. There I will be giving some practical instruction on how to expound Bible passages in an accurate and prophetic way. In this chapter I want to look at the second priority, being 'inspired by the Spirit'. I want to propose that the most effective Bible teaching is not the result of human might or human strength but rather the Spirit of the Lord. If Jesus himself needed the Spirit of the Sovereign Lord to anoint him for the task of preaching, how much more do we (Luke 4:18)! As Bible teachers we simply cannot do without the empowering presence of God.

The problem with the vast majority of books on Bible exposition is that they coach people in the natural skills needed for teaching, but they fail to emphasise sufficiently the role of the Spirit in study and communication. Those very few books that do pay some lip-service to the 'anointing of the Spirit', or to being 'clothed with power', fail to give practical advice on how to expound the Bible in a Spirit-inspired way. While they mention the Spirit in passing, we are always left with what is called 'the YBH factor': the question, *Yes! But how?*

So here are eight keys.

Key no. 1: Be filled with the Holy Spirit

If a person is to teach the Bible in the power of the Holy Spirit, then they must first be filled with the Holy Spirit themselves. We cannot expect the word of the Lord to pour out of our mouths if the power of God has not been poured into our hearts. Remember the Day of Pentecost. Peter, along with the other 119 disciples in Jerusalem, was first of all filled with God's Spirit. Having been filled, Peter stood up with the eleven and courageously spoke to the crowds gathered in the vicinity. Having been visited by tongues of fire, his own tongue caught fire. When he spoke, he pointed to various Bible passages that the Holy Spirit had burnt into his heart: parts of Joel chapter 2, Psalm 16 and Psalm 110. Peter's ability to interpret and apply these passages is in direct fulfilment of two great promises of the Old Testament:

> And I will give you a new heart with new and right desires, and I will put a new spirit in you. I will take out your stony heart of sin and give you a new, obedient heart. And I will

put my Spirit in you so you will obey my laws and do whatever I command. (Ezekiel 36:26–27)

'But this is the new covenant I will make with the people of
Israel on that day,' says the Lord. 'I will put my laws in their
minds, and I will write them on their hearts. I will be their
God, and they will be my people.' (Jeremiah 31:33)

Thanks to the coming of the Holy Spirit (in fulfilment of
these prophecies), God's word had been written on
Peter's heart. As a result, an untrained Galilean fisherman
was able to teach the Scriptures in a way that later astonished the city scholars. As Luke reports, concerning the
ministry of Peter and John in Acts 4:13: 'The members of
the council were amazed when they saw the boldness of
Peter and John, for they could see that they were ordinary
men who had had no special training.'

This incident teaches us an important lesson. We may
have all the theological education and all the communica-
tional expertise in the world, but without the Holy Spirit we
will not be an effective preacher or teacher. Indeed, Peter's
example sends a very challenging message across the centuries: it tells us that an uneducated man filled with the Holy
Spirit will be far more use to God than an educated man
filled with human learning *alone*. As a friend of mine once
wrote (and he was an Old Testament professor, no less):

I have discovered over the past seventeen years . . . that
baptism in the Spirit can often give less literate people a
much better appreciation of the message of the Bible than
three years of university education in a theology department
can give to more intellectually capable undergraduates.[1]

---

[1] John McKay, 'When the Veil is Taken Away', p. 8. Unpublished paper
on charismatic hermeneutics.

My friend here mentions 'baptism in the Holy Spirit'. I appreciate that at this point we could become bogged down in controversy. There are, after all, very different and often divisive views of the phenomenon known as baptism in the Holy Spirit. Some see it as an experience subsequent to conversion (the 'second blessing'). Others see it as part of conversion-initiation. But set aside your own doctrinal position for a moment and consider this: whatever view we adopt, the fact is God expects us to be a people filled with the Holy Spirit. Whatever our view of the exact timing of this experience, we cannot deny the testimony of the New Testament. Believers are supposed to be filled with the power of God. So be sure that you are filled with the Spirit.

Key no. 2: Keep praying for more power

One of my favourite prayers is a prayer once prayed by a Mississippi Bible teacher. He entered his pulpit one Sunday morning and said the following: 'O Lord, give thy servant this mornin' the eyes of the eagle and the wisdom of the owl; connect his soul with the gospel telephone in the central skies; illuminate his brow with the sun of heaven; possess his mind with love for the people; turpentine his imagination; grease his lips with possum oil; electrify his brain with the lightnin' of the word; put perpetual motion in his arms; fill him plumb full of dynamite of thy glory; anoint him all over with the kerosene of salvation, and set him on fire. Amen!' Now there was a man who wanted more of the fire of God in his life!

In his letter to the Ephesians, the apostle Paul encourages us to keep being filled with the Holy Spirit (5:18). The Bible teacher needs to obey this command by constantly coming before the Father and asking, 'More, Lord. Please grant me more of your Holy Spirit in my life.'

Very likely, there are two things that will prevent someone from seeking more of the power of God in their teaching ministry. The first will be pride. Pride says, 'I can teach the Bible in my own strength. I don't need more of God in my life. All that I need was provided at my conversion.' Humility, on the other hand, says, 'I can do nothing apart from the Lord. Lord, if I am to teach effectively, then I need more of your power in my life.' Pride is an expression of our independence from God. Humility is an expression of our dependence upon him. The godly Bible teacher will constantly pray, 'More, Lord.'

The other factor that inhibits praying in this way is unbelief. It may be that you do not actually believe that God's supernatural power is available today. It is just possible you have been affected by one of the greatest lies of the enemy that the power of God was for the first but not for the twenty-first century. The classic expression of this falsehood is the famous statement by Rudolf Bultmann, father of modern sceptical biblical criticism: 'One cannot use an electric light and radio, call upon modern medicine in the case of illness, and at the same time believe in the world of spirits and miracles in the New Testament.' I want you to know that there is nothing in the Bible itself to suggest that 'spirits' and 'miracles' are fictional. Furthermore, experience confirms that spirits do exist and that miracles do happen. The testimonies to come in this chapter should assure you of that. So please do not allow unbelief to drown out the cry of desperation deep within your heart. As Paul put it in Ephesians 3:20: 'By his mighty power at work within us, he is able to accomplish infinitely more than we would ever dare to ask or hope.'

Underline those two words, 'infinitely more'. You can always ask for more! As Jesus said in Luke 11:11–13:

'You fathers – if your children ask for a fish, do you give them a snake instead? Or if they ask for an egg, do you give them a scorpion? Of course not! If you sinful people know how to give good gifts to your children, how much more will your heavenly Father give the Holy Spirit to those who ask him.'

I well remember not long ago taking my whole family for a day out to a theme park. There was Alie my wife, and our four children, Philip, Hannah, Johnathan and Samuel. During the morning, my third child Johnathan came up to me, held my hand, and asked if we could go to a pizza restaurant for lunch. He had always wanted to go there and had seen that there was a restaurant in the park. So I said yes.

However, when lunchtime drew near, there was an outbreak of anarchy in my family when they realised that we were heading for a pizza restaurant. Everyone wanted to go to different places to eat. In the end, I put my foot down and announced that we were going to the place I wanted. So we moodily arrived at a restaurant that promised a wide variety. When we got there we found that the only suitable food was beefburgers and chips. So the kids ate that instead. It was overpriced and utterly revolting.

The next day I was having my prayer time and I was praying about the following Sunday night's message. I was due to preach on the subject 'The cry for Father God', out of Romans 8:15–17. One of the points I was considering was the need to ask the Father for his Spirit with the humble openness of a child. As I thought about that, I felt led to the promise of Jesus quoted above: 'You fathers – if your children ask for a fish, do you give them a snake instead?' Suddenly a sense of conviction overwhelmed me. My son Johnathan had asked for a pizza, and I had given him a burger – and a burger that tasted worse than a snake!

The next day I took him into town and bought him as much pizza as he could eat at the best pizza restaurant I could find! I have never seen him so happy.

Jesus promises that his Father loves us like no earthly father could. I am convinced that most of us are unaware of the power of simply asking the Father for the anointing of the Holy Spirit in the matter of teaching. Do we think that God does not want us to teach in the power of the Spirit? I cannot believe that! I believe his heart is bursting with a passion to pour out his fire and his favour on those who humbly ask him for help in preparing and delivering a message. All he is waiting for on our part is the longing or desire for his anointing.

Key no. 3: Receive prayer when you teach

To some this may seem obvious; to others it may come as a flash of revelation. My third key is a very simple one. Have others pray for you before, during and after your message. As Paul said in Ephesians 6:19: 'And pray for me, too. Ask God to give me the right words as I boldly explain God's secret plan that the Good News is for the Gentiles, too.' If Paul requested prayer to help him with his teaching, so should we!

I do not want to suggest that we have it all together, but in my own church there is always a prayer meeting before our Sunday evening service, and often prayer meetings before our morning ones as well. Before these services, we give ourselves to prayer. Members of our trained ministry team come to that meeting and wait on the Lord for words of revelation. Then the meeting ends with those ministering at the front receiving prayer for the Lord's anointing on their ministries.

Now there are two great reasons why the teacher needs to be at this meeting. The first is because the time of waiting on the Lord for prophetic revelation is a helpful indicator of what the Father wants to do in the meeting itself. This will either confirm the message you have prepared or lead to some potential refinements or adjustments. At the very least, it helps with the whole area of application, since the words most often refer to what the Father wants to do in the prayer ministry time after the message.

The second reason is because this meeting provides a great opportunity for the teacher to receive prayer ministry before speaking. I have found it to be essential to have trusted and trained people pray for the fire of the Spirit upon my life, and specifically for the teacher's anointing. The important thing is to receive this anointing by faith. The wonderful thing is that it is often attended by an actual experience of the fire of God as the anointing is imparted through others' prayers.

So my advice would be to receive prayer from others before speaking, and preferably with the laying on of hands. If this is not feasible for practical reasons, then ask someone to pray for you in this way during the service itself, maybe during the song or hymn before you speak. Most of the time these days, one person will be leading a meeting and another speaking. The person leading can spend a few moments praying for the anointing on the speaker's life while the congregation praises God in song.

In fact, asking for the Lord's anointing during a time of sung worship is probably the best time to offer this kind of prayer. Don't forget, it was as the prophets and teachers were ministering to the Lord in worship that the Holy Spirit ministered his revelation to them (Acts 13:2).

If receiving prayer is important before a sermon, it is just as important during it. Wherever I travel I always go in a team of at least two others, and the people I usually pick will be gifted in the area of prayer ministry and intercession. This ensures that I receive prayer before speaking, but it also ensures that I have at least one other person interceding for the anointing on my life as I speak. We would all do well to give more attention to this vital support ministry.

Finally, it is always a good thing to receive some prayer after teaching the word. Speaking personally, truly anointed teaching is a matter of perspiration as well as inspiration. You often feel exhausted as well as elated after speaking under the anointing. How important it is to be replenished after such a task! This is not selfishness. It is sense. Having given out in this way, it is so important to pray that the Father will fill you again. It is quite amazing how a simple act like this can fill you with new power and passion, so much so that you feel you could run the race all over again!

Key no. 4: Let the Holy Spirit have control

The next key to anointed teaching is a continuous openness to the prompting of the Holy Spirit. It is so important to remember the example of Jesus here. He only ever said what he heard the Father saying. He only ever did what he saw his Father doing. It was the Father's agenda that mattered, not his own, nor that of the people around him. The same needs to be true for us as well. In the teaching ministry, it is vital to become more and more adept at tracking what the Holy Spirit is doing, and going with that rather than our own plans. This may mean breaking from what we have prepared so that the Holy Spirit can minister in ways we have not planned.

There is a very interesting moment in the ministry of Jesus where we see this graphically. Jesus has just returned from a place of solitude and begins to teach. This is what Luke says:

> One day as he was teaching, Pharisees and teachers of the law, who had come from every village of Galilee and from Judea and Jerusalem, were sitting there. And the power of the Lord was present for him to heal the sick. (Luke 5:17, NIV)

As Jesus was engaged in teaching, he sensed that God's healing power was present in the place. Instead of continuing his message, Jesus responded to the leading of the Spirit and broke off his talk to minister to a paralysed man. In the unfolding story, Jesus discerns that the man needs forgiveness of sins and ministers that to him. He then heals the man of his paralysis. All of this causes consternation to the Pharisees and the teachers of the Law, who argue that only God can forgive sins. What they have not seen of course is that Jesus is God's Son. The tale concludes with everyone filled with wonder and saying, 'We have seen remarkable things today!'

There is a crucial moral here: teachers should always be led by the Spirit and should do what the Spirit wants. The apostle Paul said to all believers that we are to set our minds on what the Spirit desires (Romans 8:5). This is especially true for teachers. Sometimes we are guilty of believing that every word of our message has to be delivered and that nothing must prevent us from communicating it. But what if God wants to interrupt us? Are we going to tell the Lord of the heavens and the earth that he is not to act until we say so? We should not. If God wants us to stop speaking so that he can start acting, then we should be quiet and go with what he wants.

The real issue here is one of 'control'. Those who want to be in control of everything that is said and done will miss those moments when the Holy Spirit wants to intervene. Those who yield to God's control, who are completely abandoned to the Father's desires, will see great things.

Take the time to read the following testimony from a friend of mine in Norway. He is responsible for leading the Vineyard churches in that country and was speaking last summer at the annual summer camp for the Nordic Vineyard movement. What he describes is a perfect example of what I am talking about here:

I had prepared my message for the last evening session at the Nordic Vineyard's summer conference. I had sensed that the Lord wanted me to give some perspective to God's dealing with us as a movement over the years, and tie it to his promise of presence as we look towards the future. The core of the message was from Exodus 3:14ff., where God reveals himself as Yahweh, 'I AM', the everlasting presence, to a people who knew him as 'I was', the God of their fathers.

During the worship, the Lord started to speak to me about healing, and specifically about healing somebody with reduced hearing and somebody with a backbone that was bent. As I entered the podium with my interpreter (I had to speak in English and translation was made into Danish), I shared these few words of revelation, and suggested that we take some time to pray for these things before I started to preach. A number of people stood up from their seats, and I instructed those surrounding them to lay their hands on them and invite the Holy Spirit to come and heal them in Jesus' name.

Suddenly, my interpreter started to speak on her own, saying something about a heat in her ear and that she thought she was getting healed. She then asked if someone else could come and interpret! A little confused about what really was going on (I couldn't hear her well because of the sound system), I laid my hand on her ear and offered to pray for her. She then commented on the heat disappearing. As I moved on in my story, she again interrupted by saying over the microphone, 'Sorry, I didn't mean to get healed right now . . .' The crowd of people immediately broke into laughter. Her hearing was fine, and we continued the meeting.

The next morning, her husband came up to me, wanting to tell me what had happened. Her ear had been totally blocked because of an infection that had caused a tremendous swelling. Before the meeting, he had not been able to look into her ear, and now it was totally open, just like the other one. He was really excited about what God had done!

Another healing that had occurred during the same meeting was reported to me about an hour afterwards. A woman came up to me in the bookstore and told me that her backbone had been bent. As her husband prayed for her during the meeting, he watched it straighten up, and bend slightly over to the other side. She said that even her son, when they came back to their tent after the meeting, commented on the back looking different! Also, Ingrid, one of our leaders, had sat along with her four-year-old daughter, Martine, next to a woman who had stood up for prayer. As Ingrid and Martine laid their hands on the woman's neck, the woman suddenly exclaimed, 'I feel weightless.' She had not been able to bend her neck for over ten years, and now it was perfectly flexible.

This is a wonderful example of the importance of being flexible and going with the Father's agenda. Per-Christian, the speaker, had prepared a teaching message. But he sensed that the power of the Lord was present to heal, so he broke off the message and ministered healing in Jesus' name. Per-Christian eventually completed his message, but he also fulfilled a larger agenda. He ended up not only saying what he heard the Father saying, but also doing what the Father was doing. In the process, the Spirit confirmed the word – that God is I AM not I WAS!

Key no. 5: Eagerly desire the spiritual gifts

Paul, in his first letter to the Corinthians, commands us to desire the special abilities the Spirit gives (1 Corinthians 14:1). It is supremely important for the Bible teacher to obey this scripture and to seek other gifts that complement the gift of teaching. In 1 Corinthians 12:8–10, Paul gives a list of nine of these grace-gifts:

> To one person the Spirit gives the ability to give wise advice; to another he gives the gift of special knowledge. The Spirit gives special faith to another, and to someone else he gives the power to heal the sick. He gives one person the power to perform miracles, and to another the ability to prophesy. He gives someone else the ability to know whether it is really the Spirit of God or another spirit that is speaking. Still another person is given the ability to speak in unknown languages, and another is given the ability to interpret what is being said.

One important thing to appreciate about the teaching gift is that it does not function in isolation from all the other grace-gifts. If we simply take the list above, it is clear that at least some of these (if not the majority) are important for teaching. Indeed, I would propose that there is a cluster of gifts that relate to the teacher's role. In fact, the teacher needs to be open to using most of the gifts mentioned in Paul's list in 1 Corinthians 12, particularly wisdom, knowledge, faith, healing, miracles, prophecy and discernment:

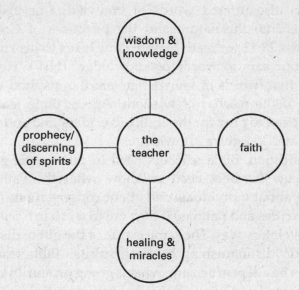

As I have shown in my book *Know Your Spiritual Gifts*, the word of wisdom and the word of knowledge are primarily 'teaching' gifts.[2] As Jesus exercised his teaching ministry, the Holy Spirit often gave him words of wisdom.

---

[2] M. Stibbe, *Know Your Spiritual Gifts* (Zondervan, 2000), chapters 1 and 2.

These utterances were expressed in the form of wise one-liners and pithy sayings. Jesus was not the first in Scripture to exercise this God-given ability. Daniel evidently excelled in this gift, and we find many wisdom sayings in the book of Proverbs, where we read that 'a person's words can be life-giving water; words of true wisdom are as refreshing as a bubbling brook' (18:4). Bible teachers today need to aspire to 'words of wisdom' more than the wisdom of words. A wise saying inspired by the Holy Spirit is indeed like life-giving water.

Jesus also uttered words of knowledge or inspired insights into the nature and the purposes of God. In Proverbs 23:12 we read, 'Apply your heart to instruction and your ears to words of knowledge' (NIV). Here, it seems that 'words of knowledge' are the inspired utterances of the teacher of wisdom. Again, Bible teachers today need to pray for the ability to understand and communicate God-given knowledge.

In addition, Bible teachers need to pursue the gift of prophecy. Teachers need to know what the Father is saying about individuals and about congregations (even towns, cities and nations) if they are to teach in a relevant and revelatory way. The same is true of the gift of discernment or 'distinguishing between spirits'. Bible teachers need to be adept at sensing what is going on spiritually as they teach. Jesus often received prophetic insight into the people he was teaching, and he also knew in his heart where people were coming from spiritually.

Healing and miraculous works are also important to the teacher. I find it absolutely essential to ask a simple question of myself every time I prepare a sermon: Does this message lead into prayer ministry? We always call people forward to receive prayer with the laying on of hands in our services, usually before or after the blessing at the end. Though the sermon is not the only deciding factor in calling people forward, it is perhaps the primary one. If the message does not lead into ministry in the power of the Spirit, then it very likely will have been too cerebral and irrelevant. The teaching – along with prophetic words given by the congregation – should result in the transformation of human lives. In my experience, the following kinds of things will usually be the focus of such ministry: salvation, rededication, repentance and forgiveness, reconciliation issues, physical healing, inner healing, deliverance, empowering for service, obeying a call to missions, worry, work issues, and so on. When these sorts of things occur, gifts of healing and miraculous works are required.

So the Bible teacher not only needs to desire gifts like the words of wisdom and knowledge (which directly relate to the teaching ministry). Other gifts should be prayed for too. Gifts like prophecy and discernment, healing and miracles, are also in the remit of the teacher's task. Though often these will be exercised corporately (through prophetic people in the congregation and ministry team members), the Bible teacher should not neglect these 'power gifts' but be like Jesus, prepared to use other God-given abilities alongside the teaching gift. In the life of Jesus and his disciples, we see a wonderful marriage of message and miracles, words and works. As Bible teachers, we need to learn to flow from the one to the other.

To do this, we are going to need the gift of faith. The gift of faith is the special, supernaturally given confidence that God is going to work powerfully in spite of the evidence of what we see. The truth is, the evidence of our eyes is very often not compelling grounds for believing that God is going to act in a mighty way. Often as Bible teachers we meet blank faces, yawning mouths and drooping heads. On the surface of it, the task of expounding the Scriptures looks pointless. The exercise of other gifts like prophecy appears to be a waste of time. Our feelings say, 'Give up and go home.' Faith says, 'Persevere; God is sovereign and is changing lives beyond what you can see with your own eyes.'

I think one of the most striking examples of this was brought to my attention quite recently. I was speaking at the Welsh National Prayer Breakfast and was drinking a cup of coffee in the break. A tall, well-spoken man in a pinstriped suit came up to me and asked for a chat. We walked out into the sunlit garden of the large house where the conference was being held and he began to share his story. He told me of a daughter of his called Rachel who had been badly treated by her husband. She had had several children by him and then he had walked out on her. She was not a Christian at the time. A few weeks later, she was on her own in the car, driving somewhere, when she had a very serious accident. The car was a write-off and she was rushed to Accident and Emergency. Her pelvis had been crushed and she had broken a number of bones. It was thought that she might not live but mercifully she pulled through. A few weeks later, a friend of the family visited her in hospital and led her to the Lord. Rachel had found her salvation. She was still, however, very poorly.

Some time later, she returned home and rejoined her daughters. She was a shadow of her former self, no longer able to walk without difficulty, her pelvis so injured that she stood at an angle. One Sunday, her father and mother visited her. They offered to take their grandchildren to church. Rachel agreed but said that she was not well enough to go herself. The father told her that was quite all right but that he had a tape with him that he would like her to listen to while they were all at church. The tape was a teaching by Jack Deere entitled 'The Healing Ministry of Jesus'. Rachel agreed somewhat reluctantly, and the others went on their way.

Over the next hour, Rachel listened to Jack teaching from the Bible on how Jesus healed people in his earthly ministry and how he still heals people today. At the end of Jack's message, the tape kept running and it included Jack's invitation for people to come forward. He himself had only one prophetic word that evening: 'pelvic realignment'. Now I do not know whether anyone responded at the actual meeting but Rachel, sitting in a far-away flat about a year after the message, struggled to her feet. As she walked forward towards the bathroom, the power of God came upon her and she was instantly healed. Her pelvis, which months before had been crushed in a car accident, was sovereignly and completely restored. The remarkable thing about all this is that the father (the one who was telling this story) was a retired medical consultant. More than that, he had at the time been attending a large, conservative evangelical church that did not believe the gifts of healing were for today. So real was this miracle that he was able to verify it as an expert medic (with X-rays), and it was enough to move him from scepticism to faith in the area of the gifts of healing and miracles.

The reason I tell this story is first because I believe there is value in recording our teaching messages, and second, because I can well imagine that Jack Deere might have wondered whether his personal prophecy had been accurate. When he said the words 'pelvic realignment', did anyone come forward in response to that specific word? I don't know. But whatever the situation in Jack's meeting, he exercised the gift of faith. He spoke something that he believed was from God and through which God was going to act in mighty power. All of us who exercise a Bible teaching ministry should take note and learn from this. We need to desire and to exercise other spiritual gifts in support of the teaching gift, especially the gift of faith. And perhaps we should have our sermons recorded as well!

Key no. 6: Remember there's a war on

We often forget that teaching is engaging in spiritual warfare. In Jesus' ministry, teaching was a weapon. Through the authority of his words (as well as the power of his works) the kingdom of God advanced forcibly. Every time Jesus taught, the reign of God was extended. Authoritative teaching was one of his primary weapons for combating the effects of the kingdom of darkness. Through his message, as well as through his miracles, Jesus destroyed the devil's work.

Preaching and teaching are accordingly weapons of our spiritual warfare. The apostle Paul knew this all too well. Writing about the ministry of preaching and teaching, he wrote these words:

> The weapons we fight with are not the weapons of the world. On the contrary, they have divine power to demolish strongholds. We demolish arguments and every pretension that sets itself up against the knowledge of God, and we take captive every thought to make it obedient to Christ. (2 Corinthians 10:4–5, NIV)

Bible teachers should take this very seriously. Teaching God's word with authority and power is one of the primary weapons for demolishing every wrong mindset that opposes the true knowledge of God. Given that this is the case, we should remember there is a war on and ensure that we pray and prepare accordingly.

An example of the power of Bible teaching may help us here. Not long ago, David Devenish from New Frontiers International was speaking in our church. He has written an excellent book called *Demolishing Strongholds*.[3] He mentioned a time when he was preaching in India. A couple came up to him after he had finished and asked him to pray for them. They explained that they could not have children. David asked why, and the woman replied, 'Because I killed a cobra when I was a teenager.'

Here is a classic example of wrong thinking, or a mindset that functions as a stronghold. The couple were living in bondage because of a cultural superstition concerning snakes. David ministered freedom to them by first teaching them the truth and then praying for deliverance in Jesus' name. The stronghold was immediately demolished and the couple had their first baby a year later.

When you hear a story like this, you realise that teaching biblical and kingdom truths is indeed spiritual warfare. That being the case, those called to continue Jesus' teaching ministry ought to be alert. There is an adversary who will not want us to hear God in our preparation and will certainly not want us to declare God's word in the pulpit. He will do everything in his limited power to prevent us from teaching with spiritual authority and ministering with spiritual power.

---

[3] D. Devenish, *Demolishing Strongholds* (Authentic Publishing, 2000).

The Bible teaches that the devil is a thief who wants to steal, kill and destroy (John 10:10). Bible teachers should be on the alert here. The enemy is absolutely terrified of teachers who expound the word of God with the fire of the Spirit burning in their hearts. He knows that the strongholds he has over people's thinking will be demolished in an instant through the declaration of God's truth. It is the truth that sets us free, after all (John 8:32). Given that this is so, Bible teachers need to be on maximum alert in their ministry. The devil will want to destroy our gift. We should therefore be aware of his schemes and be constantly vigilant.

Here are just some of the ways in which the devil will attack a Bible teacher:

- through questioning the authority of God's word
- through lies about your gifts and calling
- through distraction and confusion
- through criticism and curses
- through a fear of your congregation
- through dulling or killing the prophetic in you
- through overwork (denying you proper preparation time)
- through bitterness, anger and unforgiveness
- through unbelief born of rationalist scepticism
- through temptation in the areas of money, sex and power

Through these and other means, the devil will try to stop you teaching with fire. The good news is that we have nothing to fear. He who is in us (Jesus) is greater than he who is in the world (the devil).

So we need to remember that there is a war on. The

apostle Paul describes the sword of the Spirit as 'the word of God' (Ephesians 6:17). In Hebrews 4:12, the writer says that 'the word of God is full of living power. It is sharper than the sharpest knife, cutting deep into our innermost thoughts and desires. It exposes us for what we really are.' To teach the word of God is to wield an incisive double-edged sword. If we are to teach with fire, if we are to use the sword with dexterity, then we will need to be on our guard. We will need to pray daily for God's protection upon the message that is growing inside us. Remember, the devil loves to kill the unborn. If he can destroy the word before it is birthed, then he will be delighted. We must not give him that opportunity. We must resist the devil and guard the message from conception to birth. That way, we will be able to teach with fire.

Key no. 7: Watch your life and doctrine

From time to time, every Bible teacher should reread Paul's two letters to Timothy. They are full of challenging reminders for the minister of the word of God. Right up there among the most important of Paul's instructions to his protégé is 1 Timothy 4:16: 'Keep a close watch on yourself and on your teaching. Stay true to what is right, and God will save you and those who hear you.'

If Bible teachers are to keep the fire of God burning strong, then they must keep a careful eye on both their beliefs and their behaviour. They must maintain doctrinal purity and moral purity. This means first of all guarding against false teaching. This is particularly important as the return of the Lord Jesus grows nearer. As Paul warns: 'Now the Holy Spirit tells us clearly that in the last times some will turn away from what we believe; they will follow lying spirits and teachings that come from demons' (1 Timothy 4:1). What a stark warning that is. We must be on our guard against 'lying spirits' and 'teachings that come from demons'. All Bible teachers need to keep their teaching sound and true. The enemy wants to deceive people with falsehood and error. Even the most able teachers are vulnerable if they do not obey Paul's call to be watchful against deception.

One of the most disturbing and destructive cases of this kind of deception I have ever come across occurred in the late 1990s in Scandinavia. A large church was split and almost destroyed by a man seemingly converted from a New Age background.

The senior pastor of the church in question had been praying for revival for a long time and felt that this was it. Certainly, the stories of people being saved and healed were very dramatic. The numbers of those reported to be coming to faith were also very impressive. The fact that the new converts were formerly unchurched New Agers also sounded hopeful. Furthermore, the person at the epi-centre of this movement had an extraordinary ability to see into people's lives and to speak about hidden things.

The pastor became intimately involved with the inner core of this group. However, over a period of time, disturbing views started to emerge. The leaders began to teach that the Bible was not necessary because you could receive revelation directly from the Father – revelation that was 100 per cent accurate. This knowledge was received during trances experienced by specially gifted people in the leadership.

Not surprisingly, having left Scripture behind, unbiblical practices started to appear. The most blatant of these was the view that men could have two wives – one by legal marriage, and a 'soul wife' from within the movement. Sadly, the pastor's marriage subsequently broke up. This was tragic not only because of the dreadful unhappiness it caused but because his wife had been converted out of a New Age background many years before and had discerned all along that there were very mixed spirits at work here.

How easy it is to be deceived! Bible teachers need to watch their doctrine closely. Similarly, we need to attend to lifestyle issues. Paul lays out the ten commandments for an elder–teacher in 1 Timothy 3:2–5:

1. 'An elder must be a man whose life cannot be spoken against.'
2. 'He must be faithful to his wife.'
3. 'He must exhibit self-control, live wisely, and have a good reputation.'
4. 'He must enjoy having guests in his home.'
5. He 'must be able to teach'.
6. 'He must not be a heavy drinker or be violent.'
7. 'He must be gentle.'
8. He must be 'peace loving'.
9. He must not be someone who 'loves money'.
10. 'He must manage his own family well, with children who respect and obey him.'

I find that a very challenging list. I am particularly challenged by the second commandment, about cultivating a faithful and harmonious relationship with my wife. I have learned over the years that I can have an argument with my wife and go to London Bible College and deliver a lecture and it will not affect me. On the other hand, I can have an argument with my wife and go to my Sunday meeting to teach from the word and I will be totally ineffective. If I am to keep on good terms with the Spirit, I must keep on good terms with my wife! No wonder Paul encourages us to watch our behaviour as well as our beliefs. Doctrinal and moral purity are essential for the Bible teacher. As Paul says in 2 Timothy 1:13: 'Hold on to the pattern of right teaching you learned from me. And remember to live in the faith and love that you have in Christ Jesus.'

Key no. 8: Always seek to magnify Jesus

The last key is the most important of all. If a person wants to be an effective and anointed Bible teacher then they must always seek to glorify the Son of God in what they do and say. In John's Gospel, we read that one of the ministries of the Spirit is to give glory to Jesus. As Jesus says to his disciples in John 16:13–14:

> When the Spirit of truth comes, he will guide you into all truth. He will not be presenting his own ideas; he will be telling you what he has heard. He will tell you about the future. He will bring me glory by revealing to you whatever he receives from me.

When was this promise fulfilled? On the Day of Pentecost. When God poured out his Holy Spirit on the disciples, that same Spirit brought glory to Jesus. The means by which this occurred was through preaching and teaching. The apostle Peter stood up and delivered a message in which Jesus Christ was the central theme and the exclusive focus. He begins with the words: 'People of Israel, listen! God publicly endorsed Jesus of Nazareth by doing wonderful miracles, wonders, and signs through him, as you well know' (Acts 2:22). And he ends: 'So let it be clearly known by everyone in Israel that God has made this Jesus whom you crucified to be both Lord and Messiah!' (Acts 2:36). As Peter preaches under the anointing of the Holy Spirit, he finds one thing after another to say about Jesus. Each one serves the same goal of bringing glory and honour to the name and the person of Jesus Christ. Peter himself is barely noticeable. It is for this reason that Peter's message is so extraordinarily powerful. At the end of it, three thousand people are born again and baptised.

I believe there is a crucial message here. It can be summed up in the words of the apostle Paul, who said in 2 Corinthians 4:5: 'We don't go around preaching about ourselves; we preach Christ Jesus, the Lord.' Teachers who focus on themselves invariably communicate out of the flesh rather than the Spirit. Teachers who focus on the Lord Jesus Christ invariably communicate out of the Spirit, not the flesh.

When we magnify the Lord Jesus Christ (and not ourselves) in our teaching, we are more likely to be operating in the Spirit's power than at any other time. I have noticed many times an interesting dynamic in my experience of teaching. I can begin and continue a message but not really be aware of the anointing of the Holy Spirit. But whenever I have chosen to exalt Jesus, to lift him up in the estimation of my hearers, there has been a definite and noticeable increase in the power of God on my life, on the message and in the congregation. When teachers spontaneously begin to celebrate the majesty of Jesus, it is as if the wind of God blows upon the fire in their hearts, leading to an increase in passion and revelation. The motto of the Bible teacher should therefore be that of John the Baptist: 'He must become greater and greater, and I must become less and less' (John 3:30).

Eight keys to anointed teaching

So there are eight practical keys for anointed Bible teaching. What do I mean by the word 'anointed'? Here is what R. H. Hughes says:

> The word 'anointing' is . . . used to set forth the divine element of preaching, that which pricks the human heart and conscience, that which burns the word first into the minister's heart and then into the consciousness of the listener, and without which the mere human words become powerless and ineffective.

If you and I want to teach the Bible in the fire of God's Spirit, we cannot do without the anointing. Charles Spurgeon once said that 'it were better to speak six words in the power of the Holy Ghost than to preach seventy years of sermons without the Spirit'. How we need the Spirit's fire! How we need to be

F = Faithful to the Scriptures
I = Inspired by the Spirit
R = Relevant to our audience
E = Enthusiastic in the delivery

As John Wesley once said, 'When you go out to preach, don't worry about how to gain an audience. Get on fire, and people will come to watch you burn.'

Question time

1. *Be filled with the Holy Spirit*
   Are you experiencing the power of God in your life and ministry?
2. *Keep praying for more power*
   Are you praying for a regular increase in God's anointing on your teaching ministry?
3. *Receive prayer when you teach*
   Is it a priority for you to have people pray for you before, during and after you speak?
4. *Let the Holy Spirit have control*
   Are you flexible enough to sense and follow what the Holy Spirit desires as you speak?
5. *Eagerly desire the spiritual gifts*
   Are you pursuing other gifts that will help you in your teaching ministry (like prophecy and healing)?
6. *Remember there's a war on*
   Are you praying for victory and breakthrough in your preparation and delivery of each message?
7. *Watch your life and doctrine*
   Are you keeping on good terms with the Holy Spirit in the matter of your beliefs and behaviour?
8. *Always seek to magnify Jesus*
   Are you exalting yourself or are you giving glory to the name and the person of Jesus?

4

Expounding the Bible

Preparing for a long trip, a traveller said to his friend: 'I am just about packed. I only have to put in a guidebook, a lamp, a mirror, a microscope, a telescope, a volume of fine poetry, a few biographies, a package of old letters, a book of songs, a sword, a hammer and a set of books I have been studying.'

'But,' the friend replied, 'you can't get all that into your bag.'

'Oh, yes,' replied the traveller, 'it doesn't take much room.' He placed his Bible in the corner of the suitcase and closed the lid.

If there is one book I want with me at all times as a teacher it is the Bible. For one thing, it is a whole library of books (66 in all) compressed into one volume. For another thing, it really is a guidebook, a lamp, a microscope and a telescope, and a whole lot more besides. Most importantly of all, the Bible is God's word. It contains God's instructions on what to believe and how to behave. As a child once said to his father: 'I know what the Bible means.'

'What does it mean, son?'

'That's easy, Daddy. It stands for Basic Information Before Leaving Earth!'

The person gifted to be a teacher in the church will not be true to their calling unless they study and expound what the Bible says. A teacher in the church is a *Bible* teacher. While the prophet relies on dreams, visions, pictures, impressions and thoughts, the teacher relies on texts. This does not mean that the prophet ignores the Bible any more than it means the teacher ignores prophecy. Rather, it highlights the raw material of the respective gifts: immediate revelation in the case of the prophet, and the written word of God in the case of the teacher.

The book of the Lord

Why is the Bible so important? The Bible really is our 'basic information before leaving earth'! Thomas Carlyle put it more comprehensively a long time ago when he said:

> The Bible is the truest utterance that ever came by alphabetic letters from the soul of man, through which, as through a window divinely opened, all men can look into the stillness of eternity, and discern in glimpses their far-distant, long-forgotten home.

The Bible is divine revelation expressed through inspired human authors. The Bible is the Father's book. It is a gift from our Father in heaven, revealing his heart, his plans, his words, his deeds and his ways. Every time we read this book it truly is like coming home. It is a foretaste of that day when we will enter heaven's living-room, sit in the presence of the Father, and talk with him face to face. For that reason alone, it is the most precious book on earth.

My father died in January 1997. I owe so much to him, humanly speaking. He and my mother were responsible for adopting my sister and me. All through my life, my father constantly stressed how pleased he was that he had chosen me, and how proud he was of me (even when I had achieved nothing in particular!). He was an inspiration to me and to many others, not least in the very calm, wise and affirming words he would utter. His death in 1997 hit me very hard. Suddenly, there was no Dad to talk to at the other end of a telephone. Most painful of all, the letters stopped. Never again would I receive those wonderful, handwritten letters overflowing with unconditional affection.

After my father's death, I began to see things differently. Priorities changed. My perspective on life altered. One of the things that changed was my attitude to a book Dad had written. The book had originally been published just after the Second World War. It was a very moving account of his time as a young lieutenant in the Royal Sussex Regiment, fighting behind enemy lines in Burma. It told of his two years as a prisoner of war in Rangoon jail. Its title was *Return Via Rangoon*.

In the 1990s my brother lovingly set about republishing this book and my father experienced the joy of seeing it in a brand new edition with a brand new jacket. As a family, we all rejoiced with Dad that his book was available to the public once again. All of us reread it in its new format and secured signed editions for the grandchildren.

Today, this book is my most precious possession after the Bible. Whenever I pick it up, I am conscious that I am not just reading a record of my father's deeds but I am also experiencing once again something of his warm and gracious heart. Although I cannot see my father face to face, I can know something of his thoughts and feel something of his love. Dad's book is highly prized in our family for that reason.

The Bible is also 'Dad's book'. It is the record of our heavenly Father's acts in history but it is also a window onto his heart. He is in heaven. We are here on the earth. A great divide separates us from seeing one another face to face. One day we will be together. In the meantime, the Bible is one of the gifts God has given us to know him and to hear him. Every time we read a passage of Scripture it is like receiving a letter from heaven. The Bible is not an out-of-date relic. It is the Father's living word.

The Lord of the book

It follows from all of this that teachers cannot and must not study the Bible as if it were just like any other book. We cannot treat it as an ancient text with no contemporary relevance. Nor can we examine it in a detached and cerebral way. Many people in Jesus' day were scholars of the Old Testament Scriptures. They knew the book of the Lord but they did not know the Lord of the book. As Jesus said to some of his Jewish contemporaries: 'You search the Scriptures because you believe they give you eternal life. But the Scriptures point to me! Yet you refuse to come to me so that I can give you this eternal life' (John 5:39–40). Jesus judged the teachers of his own day for their lack of insight. Those of us who teach today need to be vigilant too. As the apostle James put it: 'Dear brothers and sisters, not many of you should become teachers in the church, for we who teach will be judged by God with greater strictness' (James 3:1).

I cannot emphasise more strongly that the Bible is the Father's book; it is all about his Son, Jesus, and we need the Holy Spirit if we are going to understand it. In other words, nothing short of a Trinitarian reading will be necessary if we are going to be effective teachers. We need to study the Bible in a devotional way, reverencing the Scriptures as the Father's gracious self-revelation to us. We need to study the Bible in a relational way, recognising that its subject is the Son of God, Jesus Christ, and that we can know him personally today. And we need to study the Bible in an inspirational way, asking the Holy Spirit who inspired the Bible to illuminate its pages in our hearts as well as our heads.

Perhaps an illustration will help at this point. There was once a Shakespearean actor who was known everywhere for his one-man show of readings and recitations from the classics. He would always end his performance with a dramatic reading of Psalm 23 (AV). Each night, without exception, as the actor began his recitation – 'The Lord is my shepherd; I shall not want' – the crowd would listen attentively. And then, at the conclusion of the psalm, they would rise in thunderous applause in appreciation of the actor's incredible ability to bring the verses to life.

But one night, just before the actor was to offer his customary recital of Psalm 23, a young man from the audience spoke up: 'Sir, do you mind if tonight I recite Psalm 23?' The actor was quite taken back by this unusual request, but he allowed the young man to come forward and stand upfront and centre-stage to recite the psalm, knowing that the ability of this unskilled youth would be no match for his own talent.

With a soft voice, the young man began to recite the words of the psalm. When he was finished, there was no applause. There was no standing ovation as on other nights. All that could be heard was the sound of weeping.

The audience had been so moved by the young man's recitation that every eye was full of tears. Amazed by what he had heard, the actor said to the youth, 'I don't understand. I have been performing Psalm 23 for years. I have a lifetime of experience and training, but I have never been able to move an audience as you have tonight. Tell me, what is your secret?'

The young man humbly replied, 'Well sir, you know the psalm . . . but I know the Shepherd.'

A person can stand in the pulpit and tell you what the Bible meant in its original historical setting, but that is not Bible teaching. That is lecturing. Teaching the Bible is something altogether more glorious than that. It is the product of a person who knows not just the book of the Lord but also the Lord of the book. It is the fruit of a relational and revelatory reading of the written word of God. No congregation wants teachers who merely conduct a verse-by-verse analysis of a passage in a dry, intellectual way. People want to hear teachers who know and love Jesus and who are able to hear what the Lord is saying through the text. As A. W. Tozer once said:

> If a man has only correct doctrine to offer me, I am sure to slip out at the first intermission to seek the company of someone who has seen for himself how lovely is the face of him who is the Rose of Sharon and the Lily of the Valley. Such a man can help me, and no one else can.

Bible teaching is therefore more than a matter of truth; it is also a matter of experience. It is more than a matter of the head; it is also a matter of the heart. It is more than just a matter of the word; it is a matter of the Spirit. Unless we remember this, our audiences will not be fed; they will be fed up.

The Spirit and the word

With this vital warning in mind, let us now turn to the practicalities of expounding the Bible. It is my personal conviction that teaching should take the form of expounding what the Bible says in the power of the Holy Spirit. If this is to happen, we must employ a hermeneutic of affection; we must study God's book with the fire of his love burning in our hearts. In short, we must be a people of the Spirit and the word.

In Chapter 1 I defined the gift of teaching as 'the God-given ability to instruct believers in a biblical and a revelatory way'. By using the word 'biblical' I was stressing the importance of basing everything we teach on what the Bible says. By using the word 'revelatory' I was highlighting the importance of teachers being enabled by God to discern the prophetic significance of the Bible for today. It is simply not enough to explain what the passage meant to its original author in their original situation. The teacher must go beyond this and show how God is speaking to us now through the words of this passage. As I wrote in Chapter 1, life change occurs when the teacher combines information with revelation.

INFORMATION + REVELATION = TRANSFORMATION

We should constantly keep before our minds the statement made by D. L. Moody that 'the Bible was not given to increase our knowledge but to change our lives'. The proper purpose of Bible teaching is not just to give information. Rather, it is to lead to the transformation of human lives through the imparting of revelation. Put another way, the purpose of Bible teaching is to conform both the teacher and the audience to the likeness of Jesus. As Paul put it in 1 Timothy 1:5: 'The purpose of my instruction is that all the Christians there would be filled with love that comes from a pure heart, a clear conscience, and sincere faith.'

If the transformation of human lives is to be achieved, then teachers need first of all to expound the Bible. Speaking personally, I am committed to the principles of 'expository' sermons. Expository teaching involves starting with a Bible passage and letting that dictate your teaching. It involves using Bible commentaries and other tools to discover what the passage meant to its first author and readers. It involves studying a text in its context, both historical and literary. It also means highlighting the leading biblical principle-in a passage and making that the focal point of the sermon. Expounding the Bible is accordingly the result of intensive literary, historical and grammatical study of a passage, verse by verse.

The advantages of this kind of teaching ministry are many. It first of all ensures that the Bible has priority and pre-eminence in the forming of the message. The text produces the topic of the message, rather than the topic the text. We may call this the advantage of *authority*. It gives the Bible first place in our thinking.

Secondly, expository teaching forces the teacher to discipline themselves in the whole area of Bible study and meditation. There is simply no room for laziness when it comes to this kind of teaching ministry. You cannot just show up on a Sunday and teach what you have not thoroughly prepared. You have to know your Bible and you have to have examined your passage verse by verse. You have to meditate and ruminate before you can 'sermonate'! Although you may deliver your message with minimal or even no notes, the preparation will have involved a rigorous process of biblical interpretation. The second great gain of expository teaching is therefore the advantage of *discipline*.

The third great gain is the advantage of *relevance*. I never cease to be amazed by the relevance of God's word. Expounding a book of the Bible in a series is a constant source of surprise on this score. I am currently preaching my way through Mark's Gospel. Every week, the Lord speaks through the set passage in the most remarkable ways. The other week I reached Mark 10, which begins with a passage about divorce. I am not sure I would ever have chosen to teach on this subject, but I could not avoid it in this series. In the event, it turned out to be the message of the hour for many couples in our church.

This relates to the fourth gain, the advantage of *variety*. Expounding a Bible book passage by passage or chapter by chapter keeps you from being repetitive in your subject matter. It forces you to deal with topics you would not normally confront (as we have just seen above) and it also keeps you from boring your people to death by preaching the same subject every week (albeit in a different guise).

For all these reasons, and no doubt others, there are great gains to systematic expository teaching. But there are some losses as well. The dangers of this approach are that the teacher ends up being very strong on interpretation but very weak on application. I have sat through many sermons that have really been no different from an academic lecture in a university department of biblical studies. Teaching like this can be too closely argued, too complex, too cerebral. It is very often a mind-to-mind rather than a heart-to-heart form of communication, and it does not result in life change. Furthermore, it can become very boring and lead to weariness on the part of the congregation, especially if the teacher spends too long in the same book. Indeed, I once heard of a preacher who spent his entire ministry, fifty years of it no less, teaching his way through the book of Job. When he began, his church had 5,000 members. When he finished, it only had 50! Obviously, you can go too far!

Expository teaching can only be truly effective if a second dimension is added, the dimension of the Spirit's power. Expounding the Bible is one of the primary values of my ministry, but it must be exposition done prophetically. I want to be a man of the Spirit and the word. I want to study the Bible and I want to explain the meaning of Bible passages to my hearers. But I want to make sure that I move beyond what each verse meant in its own day to what it means prophetically today. Expository teaching as it has traditionally been understood is inadequate for this task. If it is to meet the challenge, it must have a prophetic edge to it. It is the Holy Spirit who inspired the Bible and it is the Holy Spirit who illuminates the Bible. If we are going to be strong in the area of application, we are going to need the Holy Spirit.

Teaching as bridge building

Before I explain how to expound a Bible passage in the power of the Spirit, it may help if I introduce a picture that I first heard from Rick Warren, senior pastor of Saddleback Community Church.[1]

---

[1] Rick Warren's excellent two-video training course for preaching is entitled *Preaching for Life Change* and can be purchased from www.pastors.com

Exercising a teaching ministry is really a form of bridge building. On the one side there is the ancient biblical text. On the other side is the contemporary church and today's society. In short, we have a chasm between word and world:

The task of the Bible teacher is to build a bridge across the great expanse of time that lies between the Bible and today's situation in the church and in the world. The task of interpretation alone will not build this bridge, however. Interpreting what the Bible meant to its original authors in their original situation is a component to the teaching gift but it is not the whole story. If the bridge is to be built, then the teacher will need to excel in another component to the teaching gift, namely the ability to apply the Bible to today's situation in a prophetic way. If the first component involves discerning the meaning of a Bible passage, the second involves the revelation of its significance to us and to our people. For this to happen, the teacher will need the bridge-building ministry of the Holy Spirit.

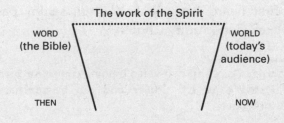

The most effective teaching is the result of inspirational interpretation and application. It is the result of intensive study of the original meaning of a passage, guided by the Holy Spirit. But then it is secondly the outcome of a process of discerning what the Holy Spirit is doing in our church and saying about our people, and applying the ancient text to these present issues and needs. Now, which of these two do you spend most time in? The word or the world? Where are your strengths? Interpretation or application? If you are all interpretation and no application, you will come across as dry and cerebral. If you are all application and no interpretation, you will run the risk of ignoring or abusing the Bible. You and I need to excel in both, and we can only do that through the revelatory work of the Holy Spirit. As Jesus said in John 14:26:

> When the Father sends the Counsellor as my representative
> – and by the Counsellor I mean the Holy Spirit – he will teach
> you everything and will remind you of everything I myself
> have told you.

We need the Holy Spirit to teach and remind *us* if we are to teach and remind *others*. While the truth of the Bible is unchanging and absolute, the form in which it must be communicated will change in every generation. We need the Spirit if we are to apply the message to today's world.

With all this in mind, let us now turn to the practice of expounding the Bible in the power of the Spirit.

Step 1: Isolate your passage

The first step is to isolate the passage that you want to teach on. Everything here depends on the kind of teaching message you are going to give. There are basically two kinds of message. There is first of all topical exposition. In a topical message, you may find yourself teaching on a subject that is particularly pertinent to your congregation. Your aim will be to teach biblical principles in this particular area. So, the topic might be 'how to witness to non-Christians', or 'how to resist temptation', or 'how to read the Bible for all it's worth'. These topics relate to basic spiritual disciplines or aspects of Christian behaviour. You may also find yourself teaching about topics that are more general, like marriage for example. These might be to a wider audience than just your church. Recently I have taught on the following subjects: 'what to do when the love runs out', 'how to have a purposeful marriage', 'three keys for a healthy relationship'. All of these have been to congregations with many visitors, including non-Christians.

In a topical exposition, my advice is not to mention a lot of Bible passages in passing if there are non-Christians present. That would be a bit like shooting with a blunderbuss. A lot of bullets would go flying in the general direction of the target, with only a few hitting. It is better to use a sniper rifle. Aim at one target using a single bullet. In other words, let one Bible passage be the basis for teaching about your topic. Only bring other passages sparingly. Cross-referencing is something I keep to the bare minimum if there are people present who are unfamiliar with the Bible.

The same does not apply when you are conducting a training seminar for Christians. In this more specific context you can afford to be more liberal with your quotations. For example, some of my most recent teaching has been for leaders on the subject of 'developing vision for the local church'. I have also recently taught a three-session module on 'prophetic evangelism', training people to use the gift of prophecy when they are with non-Christians. And I have taught a seminar on 'how to deliver the oppressed' to those training to join our prayer ministry team. In each of these sessions, I used a good number of Bible references. So you can be flexible, depending on the context, the aim of your teaching and your audience.

The second kind of message is what I call 'typical exposition'. Here we are talking about interpreting and applying a single, manageable portion of Scripture. It may be that you are in a church where the passage has already been chosen for you. If you are going through a book of the Bible, then the chances are you have the text already selected. If your church follows a lectionary, then the same applies. In that case, work within those boundaries. Having a passage fixed for you in advance in no way quenches the Spirit's fire. Jesus' first sermon was based on the set reading in his synagogue, Isaiah 61. The scroll with this reading was handed to him in the synagogue at Nazareth. Jesus read it out and said, 'This Scripture has come true today before your very eyes!' (Luke 4:21). This was a very short message, which goes to show that a sermon does not have to be eternal in order to be immortal. It was also based on a fixed reading, which goes to show that an established framework does not inhibit the Spirit's freedom. Jesus' example shows that you can speak prophetically through a predetermined passage.

It may be, however, that you have to choose the passage yourself. If this is the case, it is always best to use a text that has very recently spoken to you personally. Some of the finest sermons are those in which the teacher shares with others what the Holy Spirit has first burned on their heart. Very recently I have spoken on the following Bible passages and subjects. In every case, the Holy Spirit has fixed his light on these texts and revealed subjects that are very much on the Father's heart:

1. Psalm 78:1–8. The destiny of our nation's children.
2. Luke 10:1–12. Seven ways to transform your community.
3. Mark 1:1–8. Preparing for revival.
4. John 4:27–38. From consumerism to evangelism.
5. Leviticus 25. The King's jubilee.

Although these messages have probably been more like 'topical exposition' than 'typical exposition', they have still used a single passage of Scripture as the focus of what I felt the Lord wanted me to say.

In summary, isolate the passage you want to teach on. It may be that the passage has already been chosen, in which case submit to that. If you are given a topic, then try to stick to one passage and do that justice, especially if there are people in your audience who are not used to the names of Bible books. If you are training rather than teaching, you can mention more Bible references because your audience will almost certainly be people who already know something of the Scriptures and who are being equipped by you to minister in some practical way. If you are not given any passage or topic, then my advice is to speak from a passage that the Lord has written with particular power on your own heart.

Step 2: Look at different translations

When you have decided on the passage, the next step is to read it in different translations. The best thing is to read the passage in its original language. But not everyone can read Hebrew (the Old Testament, mostly) or Greek (the New Testament). So the next best thing to do is to read different translations of the passage in your own native language.

At this point, I would like to use a practical example. In Step 1, I mentioned the importance of isolating your passage. As I prepared this chapter, I asked the Father to quicken a passage I could use to encourage teachers. I was then drawn to some words in Matthew's Gospel, about the teacher being like a householder who brings out of his storeroom treasures new and old. As the Holy Spirit brought that to mind, I went to the version of the Bible I use most, the New Living Translation. This for me combines the virtues of accuracy and accessibility like no other contemporary version. Using a concordance, I found the exact reference in Matthew 13:52. Here is how the New Living Translation renders it:

> Then he added, 'Every teacher of religious law who has become a disciple in the Kingdom of Heaven is like a person who brings out of the storehouse the new teachings as well as the old.'

Having read this in the New Living Translation, I went to the New International Version. This renders Matthew 13:52 as follows:

> He said to them, 'Therefore every teacher of the law who has been instructed about the kingdom of heaven is like the owner of a house who brings out of his storeroom new treasures as well as old.'

As a final step, I consulted one of the old translations, the Authorised Version. The Authorised Version (also known as the King James Version) translates Matthew 13:52 as follows:

> Then said he unto them, Therefore every scribe which is instructed unto the kingdom of heaven is like unto a man that is an householder, which bringeth forth out of his treasure things new and old.

When you read different translations it is always interesting to compare how each one has rendered the original. So, for example, the NLT and NIV speak of a 'teacher of (religious) law' while the AV speaks of a 'scribe'. This is not significant in itself because the words 'scribe' and 'teacher of the law' are interchangeable. However, the next part of the statement is more important. In the NLT, the scribe is said to be 'a disciple *in* the kingdom of heaven' (my italics), while in the NIV he 'has been instructed *about* the kingdom of heaven' (my italics), and in the AV he 'is instructed *unto* the kingdom of heaven' (my italics). Clearly, there is a lack of consensus about how to translate this phrase. However, the three translations do agree on how to render the rest of the verse.

There are two major advantages of looking at different translations of the same passage. This particular discipline can first of all highlight some part of your passage that has proven difficult to translate with absolute precision. This is important because you do not want to build a major message on a shaky foundation. It can secondly give you a fresh insight into a familiar passage. Looking at different translations of the same verse is like turning a diamond in the light. A phrase, a metaphor or a sentence in one translation may not shine at all; the same phrase in a different version can impact you in an extremely powerful way.

Step 3: Study the text in depth

The key thing here is to make sure you study the passage so as to discern what the author originally meant. As the old saying goes, 'a text without a context becomes a pretext'. If we are not to abuse a passage by making it mean something that it was never intended to mean, we need to do some in-depth study using Bible commentaries. You may need to get some advice about which commentaries are most helpful for each book of the Bible. If you are familiar with Hebrew and Greek, then by and large I recommend the Word Biblical Commentaries. If you are not, but you want good scholarship nonetheless, I recommend the Pillar Commentaries on the New Testament. There are also some great devotional commentaries, such as those by Matthew Henry and William Barclay, and these I highly recommend. As you study the grammatical and historical details of the passage using these study aids, keep open to the help of the Holy Spirit. He will help you to understand the meaning of the text and he will also aid you in the discovery of its contemporary significance.

As we study a text in depth, there are five vital questions that we must ask and answer:

1. What kind of writing is this?
2. What is its context?
3. What is the subject of the passage?
4. What did the author intend?
5. What are the significant words?

Let us now go through these questions in relation to Matthew 13:52.

So, first of all, what kind of writing is this? It is a parable. Jesus has been telling parables throughout Matthew 13. He has been comparing the kingdom of heaven with a sower, wheat and weeds, a mustard seed, yeast, hidden treasure, a pearl and a fishing net. In each case, Jesus has been using a simile, 'the kingdom of heaven is like . . .'. Now Jesus concludes this section of teaching by asking his disciples, 'Do you understand?' (v. 51). They reply that they do. He then in verse 52 likens a teacher of religious law who has become a disciple of the kingdom to a generous householder. In the first part of the verse he is speaking literally: 'Every teacher of religious law who has become a disciple in the kingdom of heaven . . .' In the second part of the verse he is speaking figuratively: '. . . is like a person who brings out of the storehouse the new teachings as well as the old.' We need to adjust our response to a passage in the light of its genre.

Second, what is the context of this text? In terms of the literary context, the passage forms the conclusion of all the illustrations Jesus has been giving in Matthew 13. Up to verse 35, this teaching has been to the crowds. From verses 36 to 52, Jesus is speaking in private with his disciples.

This saying in verse 52 is the final part of this private teaching and begins with the word 'Therefore' (NIV). Whenever you see 'therefore' in a passage, ask what it is 'there for'. Clearly Jesus is summing up his teaching that preceded this saying. He is indirectly describing what he himself has been doing when he speaks about the householder bringing out treasures new and old. As Jesus teaches about the kingdom of heaven, he himself is dispensing treasure. This treasure is both old and new. Some of it is as old as Moses. Some of it is brand new. He now indicates that he wants his disciples to do likewise.

A further comment needs to be made about the historical background of this saying. One important piece of information concerns Jesus' dealings with 'scribes' or 'teachers of the law'. The scribes in Jesus' day were the guardians and interpreters of Scripture. They would often start their training at 14 and be ordained at 40. They held positions of great responsibility and prestige and many became members of the Sanhedrin. The problem with them was that their interpretations of the Law often became more important than the Law itself. Some also became proud because of their prestige and were guilty of gross hypocrisy. So Jesus warns the crowds and his disciples:

'The teachers of religious law and the Pharisees are the official interpreters of the Scriptures. So practise and obey whatever they say to you, but don't follow their example. For they don't practise what they teach'. (Matthew 23:1–3)

Now why is this historical information important to Matthew 13:52? The reason is because Jesus is here speaking about 'every teacher of religious law who has become a disciple in the Kingdom of Heaven' (NLT). This means that some scribes in Jesus' day became believers. Instead of following some particular rabbi, they chose to follow Jesus. Instead of adhering to some particular school of thought, they became subjects of the kingdom of heaven. In fact, many commentators think that this is exactly what happened to Matthew himself. His Gospel has been called 'the Teacher's Gospel', and it seems as if he has signed his own name in this verse in Matthew 13:52. The word translated 'become a disciple' is *matheeteutheis* (from the verb *matheteuein*, 'to make a disciple') and it looks very like Matthew's name (*Matthaios*)! So Jesus envisaged that there would be 'redeemed scribes' in the kingdom!

Our third question relates to the subject of this passage. Charles Simeon once said: 'I think that every sermon should like a telescope have but one object in its field.' So what is the focus of this passage? Jesus is talking here about trained teachers in the kingdom of God. He is defining what these people look like. We could say that he is providing a job profile from his own example. That being the case, the subject of the passage can now be expressed in the form of a single, simple title for our sermon. I would suggest something like 'The teacher's job description'.

Our fourth question relates to the author's intention. What did the author intend by these words in this particular context? Here we need to be accurate. We do not want to make a main point out of what the author did not intend. We need to imagine the author saying of us, 'Yes, that is exactly what I was trying to communicate.' So accuracy is the goal here. Our objective must be to respect Paul's instruction to Timothy: 'Work hard so God can approve you. Be a good worker, one who does not need to be ashamed and who correctly explains the word of truth' (2 Timothy 2:15).

At this stage, it is a great advantage to be able to understand the original language of the Bible. However, even if you do not, you can use a resource like the *PC Study Bible*, a CD ROM with everything you could possibly need to be a good teacher. It has numerous Bible translations as well as the whole Bible in its original language. It also has Bible dictionaries (so you can look up words like 'scribe') and a good number of commentaries (including Matthew Henry's, one of the best for sermon preparation). So I recommend you invest in something like this.

As we look at the meaning of the words, it is clear that the author intended to make the point that a scribe who becomes a follower of Jesus has a double blessing to offer. Not only does he have the old treasures of his former way of life as a teacher of the Law. He now also has the new treasures of his redeemed way of life as a follower of Jesus and a subject of the kingdom of heaven. This seems to be the point that Jesus is making and that the author Matthew intends by the words. The Living Bible perhaps renders the meaning (as the author intended it) most clearly: 'Those experts in Jewish law who are now my disciples have double treasures – from the Old Testament as well as from the New!' Though the Living Bible adds things that are not actually there (the reference to the Old and New Testaments) and omits things that are (the reference to the 'householder'), the 'sense' of what is meant by Jesus in this context is conveyed accurately.

What, finally, of the significant words in this passage? We have already looked at the word 'scribe' or 'teacher of the law' (*grammateus* in Greek). This word is used 24 times in Matthew's Gospel, and the greatest number of these occurrences is in Matthew 23, where Jesus describes the failings of the scribes in his own day.

The next significant word is translated 'become a disciple'. The Greek verb is *matheteuein* and is used only four times in the entire New Testament, three times in Matthew's Gospel. The most famous occasion is in Matthew 28:19: 'Therefore, go and *make disciples* of all the nations, baptizing them in the name of the Father and the Son and the Holy Spirit' (my italics).

The next significant word or phrase is 'the kingdom of heaven'. Matthew prefers to use this phrase rather than 'the kingdom of God' but means the same thing by it. It means 'the dynamic reign of God on the earth'. Jesus clearly knew that there would be trained teachers of the Bible who would become subjects of his reign.

The next word to highlight is the word 'householder' (*oikodespotes* in Greek). This means 'the master of the house' or 'the head of a family'. Matthew uses this word six other times in his Gospel. He has already used it in chapter 13 in the parable of the wheat and weeds (see 13:27). In Matthew 20, Jesus tells a story about a householder (the parable of the vineyard workers, 20:1–16). He fashions a whole story around this figure in the parable of the landowner in Matthew 21:33–46. In Matthew 24:43 Jesus talks about the owner of a house in a parable illustrating the Second Coming. These references show that the word is significant to Matthew.

The next key word is the Greek word which means 'brings out' (in relation to treasure). This is an interesting word used some 30 times by Matthew in his Gospel. It is *ekballein*, which literally means to 'pull out', 'send out' or 'throw out'. It is often used of the demons in Matthew's Gospel, when cast out by Jesus. The householder's actions in Matthew 13:52 convey a sense of wilful, almost aggressive, generosity. He is depicted as almost throwing out his treasures. The use of this word, along with the reference to treasure, is similar to another saying of Jesus recorded in Matthew 12:35 (AV): 'A good man out of the good treasure of his heart bringeth forth [*ekballein*] good things: and an evil man out of the evil treasure bringeth forth [*ekballein*] evil things.'

This reference is also important to us because it contains another word significant to Matthew. This is the word *thesauros*, translated 'treasure', and refers to a store or chest of valuables. It is used in the saying above and it is used of the householder in Matthew 13:52, who brings out of his treasure chest 'things new and old' (AV). The word is used in Matthew 2:11 of the treasure chest of the wise men who came to the baby Jesus offering gold, frankincense and myrrh. It is used in Jesus' saying in Matthew 6:19–21 about not storing up treasure on earth but treasure in heaven. It is used a few verses before our passage, in Matthew 13:44:

> The Kingdom of Heaven is like a treasure that a man discovered hidden in a field. In his excitement, he hid it again and sold everything he owned to get enough money to buy the field – and to get the treasure, too!

The comparison between the kingdom of heaven and treasure clearly prepares for Matthew 13:52, and shows that the new treasures that the redeemed scribe has to offer have to do with God's kingdom.

In summary, the words that are significant to Matthew are:

- scribe/teacher of the law
- discipled
- kingdom of heaven

- householder
- bringing out
- treasure chest

We know these words are particularly important in Matthew 13:52 because they are important to Matthew elsewhere in his Gospel.

Step 4: Identify the timeless truths

As we move to this fourth step, we are beginning to build a bridge across the gap of centuries between the ancient word and today's world. So, as we continue to study the passage in question, we need now to be listening to what the Holy Spirit is saying to us through the text. Are there some words, phrases or sentences that are becoming luminous? Are fresh thoughts being stimulated by our interaction with the words of the Bible?

While looking at Matthew 13:52, I have given this very short passage the title 'The teacher's job description'. Out of our study of this verse we have begun to discern a number of abiding principles that apply to the teacher's ministry today. The first step is to identify what these actually are, and the second is to express them in compact, practical and motivational slogans. So, let me suggest the following.

THE TEACHER'S JOB DESCRIPTION

Slogan no. 1: Learn as much as you can

Jesus does not despise learning in this verse. He has room in his kingdom for the *grammateus*, the person who has spent years interpreting the written word of God. Have you spent time studying the Bible? Have you done any study courses on the Old and New Testaments? Have you been to Bible college? Have you continued to study the Scriptures even after you finished your ministry training or your university degree? It was Henry Ford who said, 'Anyone who stops learning is old, whether at twenty or eighty. Anyone who keeps learning stays young.' Sometimes we give the impression that learning theology or doing biblical studies is contrary to the will of God or inconsistent with reliance on the Spirit. Not so. Jesus wants scribes!

Slogan no. 2: Maintain a life of integrity

The trained Bible teacher needs to be a disciple of the kingdom of God. We must not only be students of God's word, we must also be people who have become subjects of God's rule on the earth. The scribes of old were not by and large people of transparent integrity. In fact, Jesus criticises them for not practising what they preached. Like the teacher Miss Jean Brodie, they were in effect telling the people, 'Do as I say, not as I do.' Jesus warns the crowds not to follow their example. It follows from this that the Bible teacher today is to be the exact opposite. We are to live the whole of our lives as obedient servants of the King of kings. We are to practise what we preach. We are to be a people of integrity who can say, 'Do as I say' *and* 'Do as I do.' With the apostle Paul, we need to be able to declare, 'Imitate me.' As Albert Einstein once said, 'The only rational way of educating is to be an example – if one can't help it, a warning example'. So Bible teachers need to maintain a life of integrity and purity.

Slogan no. 3: Store every gem of truth

Jesus likened the kingdom teacher to a householder who had a store of treasure. We need to record every gem of truth we learn. In your own times of personal Bible study, keep a record of every verse and every thought that strikes you. When you hear other Bible teachers, make a note of everything that impacts you as a word of wisdom or a word of knowledge. 'Wisdom is far more valuable than rubies' (Proverbs 8:11). Make sure you keep enlarging the supply of treasure in your storeroom. Be organised in your filing of everything of value and consider keeping a journal. Be a responsible householder of the things of God. 'How much better to get wisdom than gold, and understanding than silver!' (Proverbs 16:16).

Slogan no. 4: Be lavish in your generosity

Jesus taught that the teacher would be a person who literally threw out treasure. The teacher needs to be a person with a lavishly generous heart. We need to be constantly giving away the jewels of truth that the Lord has given to us. Freely we have received these things, so freely we must give them away (Matthew 10:8). The Father has been extravagant in his blessing of us (Ephesians 1:3–8). Let us be extravagant in our blessing of others. This is irrespective of whether the people are receptive or not. As Paul said to Timothy: 'Preach the word of God. Be persistent, whether the time is favourable or not. Patiently correct, rebuke, and encourage your people with good teaching' (2 Timothy 4:2).

Slogan no. 5: Keep open to fresh insights

Jesus said that the characteristic of the teacher would be the double blessing of being able to bring out new revelation as well as old. We need to be constantly open to the Holy Spirit as Bible teachers. As I said in Chapter 1, the gift of teaching is the God-given ability to instruct believers in a biblical and a revelatory way. The word 'biblical' reminds us that we are the guardians and communicators of old wisdom. The word 'revelatory' reminds us that we are to provide new insights into old words. We need the help of the Holy Spirit to bring forth new insights as well as old. The important thing is to cultivate an attitude of openness to the new. As Confucius said, 'Acquire new knowledge while thinking over the old and you may become a teacher of others'. We cannot acquire new knowledge into the old unless we are open to that. So pray for the wisdom and knowledge that are the gifts of the Spirit.

Slogan no. 6: Offer everything to the Lord

I love the picture of the *thesauros* in Matthew 13:52. I am captivated by the thought that I have a store of treasure that the Lord has deposited in my life. I am thrilled with the thought that the Father has invested such wealth in an ordinary person like me. This kind of outrageous grace makes me want to be generous too. Yet at the same time I cannot help thinking that I am to do more than give these treasures to others. I want to give them to Jesus too. I want my teaching to be an offering to the Lord himself. Like the wise men in Matthew 2:11, who brought gifts out of their *thesauros* and gave them to the infant Christ, so I want to make sure all my learning and teaching is laid at the feet of the one who gave up everything for me. When teaching, make sure you offer your ministry as an act of worship to the Lord Jesus. Do it all for him. As Paul put it in Colossians 3:17 (NIV): 'And whatever you do, whether in word or deed, do it all in the name of the Lord Jesus, giving thanks to God the Father through him.'

So then,

- learn as much as you can
- maintain a life of integrity
- store every gem of truth
- be lavish in your generosity
- keep open to fresh insights
- offer everything to the Lord

This is the 'teacher's job description' as indicated by Matthew 13:52. Put this way, it is as exciting and inspiring to us today as it must have been to Matthew in his day. Truly, the principles here are timeless.

Step 5: Ask what response is required

The fifth and final step to expounding the word in the power of the Spirit is to consider what response is called for by the text. The Bible is an extremely practical and powerful book. It is God's word, so we should not expect anything else. When we study a passage with a view to teaching it, we must always ask the question posed by the audience of Peter's first sermon, 'What should we do?' (Acts 2:37). What action might my audience need to take in response to this passage of Scripture? What life changes are being called for here? What does God want to *do* to confirm and accredit what he has *said*?

Everything here depends on the audience you are teaching, so very little can be said. The important things are to ask the question in the first place, and secondly to be as aware of the needs of your audience as you possibly can. So, for example, my study of Matthew 13:52 might one day be used in a session teaching other Bible teachers. If I use this, then I will be thinking of the following kinds of response: a call to study and train as a Bible teacher, repentance for issues of disobedience, more prophetic gifting so as to receive fresh insights, and so on. As Pentecostal writer Cheryl Bridges Johns says: 'If we truly want to know God, we must respond in loving obedience to the light he has shed on our paths. The question is, "Lord, what would you have us do in response to your word?"'

If you and I want to expound God's word in the power of the Spirit, we must isolate our passage, look at different translations, study the text in depth, identify the timeless truths and ask what response is required. In taking these steps, we must be wholly reliant on the Holy Spirit at all times. As Paul wrote:

> No one can know what anyone else is really thinking except that person alone, and no one can know God's thoughts except God's own Spirit. And God has actually given us his Spirit (not the world's spirit) so we can know the wonderful things God has freely given us. (1 Corinthians 2:11–12)

That being the case, we must be sure to do our expository work not with natural minds but with spiritual minds. We will use the full resources of biblical scholarship if we are wise. But we will not use them at the expense of the prophetic or the charismatic. God wants his Spirit and his word to be reunited in the teaching ministry. My prayer is that the five-step model offered in this chapter will help towards that great end.

QUESTION TIME

Here is a check-list for the next time you teach a message:

1. Have you isolated a passage to speak from?
2. Is God speaking to you personally through this passage?
3. Have you checked what the original language says?
4. Have you considered at least two other translations?
5. Have you studied the passage in depth?
6. Have you looked carefully at:
   - the genre of the passage
   - the context of the passage
   - the subject of the passage
   - the author's intention
   - the significant words?
7. Has the Holy Spirit excited your heart with some timeless truths?
8. Can you express these principles in a practical way?
9. Have you considered what response is called for?
10. Have you conducted the process using your natural mind alone, or with a mind and a heart on fire?

5

Preparing the Message

I remember a few years ago there was an exchange of letters in a national newspaper. The subject was the importance of preaching sermons. The first letter went something like this:

Dear Sir,

I have observed over the years how preachers lay a great deal of emphasis on the importance of preaching, and how they spend inordinate amounts of time preparing sermons. I have been a churchgoer now for over 30 years and during that time I calculate that I have heard over 3,000 sermons. However, I have realised to my horror that I cannot remember a single one of them. I wonder therefore whether the preacher's time would be more profitably spent in something more effective.

Yours faithfully . . .

A great number of letters were sent in by way of response to this, but perhaps the most telling was the following, written by a preacher:

Dear Sir,

I have been married to the same woman for over 30 years. During that time I calculate that I have eaten over 30,000 meals cooked mostly by my wife. However, I have realised to my horror that I cannot remember anything about a single one of them. Having said that, I know that I have received nutrition and nourishment from every one of them. More than that, I am convinced that without them I would have died of starvation a very long time ago.

Yours faithfully . . .

There were no more letters after this one!

Cooking and preaching

I have begun with this because I believe there are some interesting parallels between preparing a meal and preparing a sermon. The Bible itself suggests this parallel in at least four ways. First of all, it compares teaching God's people with feeding sheep. Second, we find the same word used for presenting truth that is used for presenting food. Third, there is the idea that God's word is nourishing. Fourth, we find the comparison between a diet of teaching and a diet of food.

So, first of all, there is the comparison between teaching God's people and feeding sheep. In the Old Testament, the Hebrew verb *ra'ah* means 'to feed a flock' and is used of spiritual instruction in places like Proverbs 10:21: 'The lips of the righteous nourish [*ra'ah*] many, but fools die for lack of judgment' (NIV). This same thought is carried over into the New Testament in John 21:15–17, where Jesus three times commands Peter to feed the flock:

After breakfast Jesus said to Simon Peter, 'Simon son of John, do you love me more than these?'

'Yes, Lord,' Peter replied, 'you know I love you.'

'Then feed my lambs,' Jesus told him.

Jesus repeated the question: 'Simon son of John, do you love me?'

'Yes, Lord,' Peter said, 'you know I love you.'

'Then take care of my sheep,' Jesus said.

Once more he asked him, 'Simon son of John, do you love me?'

Peter was grieved that Jesus asked the question a third time. He said, 'Lord, you know everything. You know I love you.'

Jesus said, 'Then feed my sheep.'

Second, there is the parallel between presenting truth and presenting food. Matthew tells us that Jesus told the crowds another parable (Matthew 13:24). This rather weak translation is from the NIV. The RSV perhaps puts it best: 'Another parable he put before them'. The Greek verb translated 'put before' is *paratithemi*. It is commonly used of either truth or food. So, for example, we find many occasions on which *paratithemi* is used of presenting food. In Mark 6:41, during the miracle of multiplying the bread and fish, the author writes: 'Taking the five loaves and two fish and looking up to heaven, he gave thanks and broke the loaves. Then he gave them to his disciples to set before the people' (NIV).

In addition to Matthew 13:24, Matthew uses *paratithemi* in 13:31. Paul also uses *paratithemi* in connection with teaching. In 1 Timothy 2:2 he tells his pupil: 'The things you have heard me say in the presence of many witnesses entrust [*paratithemi*] to reliable men who will also be qualified to teach others' (NIV).

The third point to mention in passing is the way in which God's word is described as nourishing. Here is just one example, from Psalm 19:9–11:

> The laws of the Lord are true; each one is fair.
> They are more desirable than gold, even the finest gold.
> They are sweeter than honey, even honey dripping from the comb.
> They are a warning to those who hear them;
> there is great reward for those who obey them.

Fourth and finally, we find in the Bible a comparison between a diet of teaching and a diet of food. This is expressed in the form of a contrast between baby food and solids. The baby food is for new believers. The solids are for mature believers. In the letter to the Hebrews (5:12–14), the writer chastises the church for the fact that they have not progressed beyond drinking milk. He argues that they should long ago have been eating a far more substantial diet:

> You have been Christians a long time now, and you ought to be teaching others. Instead, you need someone to teach you again the basic things a beginner must learn about the Scriptures. You are like babies who drink only milk and cannot eat solid food. And a person who is living on milk isn't very far along in the Christian life and doesn't know much about doing what is right. Solid food is for those who are mature, who have trained themselves to recognize the difference between right and wrong and then do what is right.

We find Paul making a very similar point in 1 Corinthians 3:1–2:

Dear brothers and sisters, when I was with you I couldn't talk to you as I would to mature Christians. I had to talk as though you belonged to this world or as though you were infants in the Christian life. I had to feed you with milk and not with solid food, because you couldn't handle anything stronger. And you still aren't ready . . .

The apostle Peter uses the same analogy in 1 Peter 2:2.

In four ways at least, then, the Bible suggests a parallel between teaching and cooking, and between learning and feeding.

In this final chapter, I want to give some practical guidelines for preparing a message. I am going to suggest to you that seven things are needed if we are to present the truth in a nourishing way:

1. Be prepared to work hard.
2. Consider what others need.
3. Decide on what to serve.
4. Read the recipe carefully.
5. Gather all your ingredients.
6. Give care to presentation.
7. Serve at the right temperature.

My prayer is that this chapter will whet your appetite and inspire you to become an extraordinary chef in the things of the Spirit!

1. Be prepared to work hard

I remember not long ago my wife having to cook for about 30 Norwegian pastors. The Lord has given my wife a great love for Norway, so she really went to town on her preparation. She prayerfully considered what kind of meal would most bless them and then set to it. She laid out a table in our chapel, where the meeting was to take place and where I was to give a talk on revival. She set the table with a lovely lace tablecloth and candles. She made a red, white and blue flower arrangement, decorated with the Norwegian and English flags. She then set out a cold Scandinavian buffet with ham and salmon, Norwegian style bread and cheese, followed by Scandinavian desserts. When our guests entered the room for the meeting, they were greeted by a glorious feast. They were truly at their ease by the time I stood up to share some Bible teaching with them.

It was quite fascinating listening to the comments afterwards. Our Norwegian friends were helped by the message I gave, but they were absolutely overwhelmed by the meal provided by my wife. When they came in and saw the care Alie had taken over the choice and presentation of the food, they were moved to tears. It conveyed to them that we valued and welcomed them, in a way far more powerful than words. I will never forget the look in some of their eyes as they said thank you at the end of the evening for all the hard work.

Preparing a message, like preparing a meal, requires hard work. Anyone who is called to be a teacher in the church needs to understand this. As much work goes into preparing a message for a Sunday service as goes into preparing a meal for a large gathering. To be sure, there are times when the Holy Spirit takes control of your life and you find yourself preaching what you have not prepared. But these occasions are really the exception rather than the rule. Most of the time, a lot of unseen background work is required, and this is part of your hidden history of righteousness before God. I call this secret service 'a loving preparation of the truth'. The key word here is the word 'love'. It is just as Keith Floyd says of the most important quality needed to be a good chef:

> There is one more thing – love. Love for food and love for those you invite to your table. With a combination of these things you can be an artist – not perhaps in the representational style of a Dutch master, but rather more like Gauguin, the naïve, or Van Gogh, the impressionist. Plates or pictures of sunshine taste of happiness and love.[1]

So be prepared to work hard. A chef has to work to a certain time schedule in order to prepare a meal. As Bible teachers we are no different. There may be many other calls on our time. There may be many other pressures we face. But these must not distract us from an unhurried and loving preparation of the truth for God's people. If you need to delegate some of your tasks so that you can make room for this priority, then do so. The important thing as a Bible teacher is to put first things first. When my wife is cooking in the kitchen, only an emergency will divert her from the business of preparing the meal. So it should be with those of us who have a ministry of teaching. It does not matter how loud the children – or members of the congregation – clamour for our attention, unless it is an emergency we must be focused on the high calling God has given us. As John Wycliffe once said:

> The highest service that we may attain to on earth is to preach the word of God. And for this cause Jesus left other works and occupied himself mostly in preaching, and thus did the Apostles . . .

---

[1] Keith Floyd, *A Feast of Floyd* (HarperCollins, 1998).

2. *Consider what others need*

When we prepare a meal, we begin by thinking of the people we are serving. This is absolutely crucial. If we serve up a meal that others cannot eat, we are failing in our duties as a good chef. Similarly, if we deliver a message that is totally irrelevant to our hearers, we are failing in our duties as a good communicator. So ask, 'What do these people need at this time?' Jesus was a great communicator because he told the people what they needed to hear, not necessarily what they wanted to hear. What do our people need to hear from God right now?

If you regularly teach in your church, I would like to ask you these questions: How well do you know your people? Are you familiar with their daily struggles? Do you know what is going on in their homes and in their hearts? Do you know what they will be doing the next day, Monday, in the workplace, or at school? Have you ever seen the 'view from the pew'?

When it comes to preparing a message, the place to start is by considering the needs of the people you are serving. These needs will fall into two basic categories: subject and style. Let us look briefly at both of these.

First of all, we will need to consider what subjects our people need to hear about. If we listen to what is really going on in people's hearts we will know what they need teaching about. Recently, I asked a medical doctor in my congregation what the ten most frequently asked questions were in his surgery. This is what he wrote back:

I have observed my patients; their questions (stated or implied) and needs over the last four days. Our population tends to be in the lower social groups, and in line with the rest of the nation many people are in severe distress. In fact, of our practice – out of

*9,200 – over 570 have received or are receiving anti-depressant
medication (taken over a 12-month period); that is 6.2 per cent.*
  Here are some of the questions/comments:

1. *He'll never change – he's just like his mother. [Can the
   leopard change his spots?]*
2. *How can I break this habit/addiction?*
3. *Why did this happen to me?*
4. *I look so ugly. [How can I feel lovely on the inside, and like
   myself?]*
5. *How can I stop family manipulation – what are my responsibilities to my family?*
6. *How will I relate to my wife in heaven?*
7. *How can I remain useful in later life when my body's decay-
   ing?*
8. *How can I cope with stress?*
9. *Comments about wars and world troubles: 'Where is it all
   going to end?'*
10. *How do I appease malevolent forces to prevent further harm
    (superstition etc.)?*

This is by no means exhaustive.

When I read this list, I thought what a great sermon series
you could fashion out of these ten FAQs (frequently asked
questions). Here is an example of how listening to your
own flock can put you in touch with the real needs of real
people. As a Bible teacher, the chances are you spend a fair
amount of time within the grounds of your church building, not interacting on an intensive and everyday level
with either Christians in the workplace or non-Christians
in your community. Keeping in close pastoral relationship
with your people is an essential requirement if you are

going to deal with the right subjects in your teaching ministry. We must listen well if we are to speak well.

The second issue is the issue of style. We may have the right subject, but this is worth little if we do not understand the best style of presentation required. Today we live in a postmodern rather than a modern context. The modernist preference for all things rational and logical has been replaced by the postmodernist preference for the emotional and intuitive. In a general sense, we need to ensure that our style of presentation is not *logos* without *pathos*, reason without passion. People today prefer story to dogma, and we need to adjust our style in the light of that.

So consider not only the subject but the style of presentation. It has been suggested that people can broadly speaking be divided into two types: bookish and non-bookish:

Bookish people . . .	*Non-bookish people . . .*
think in words	think in pictures
think in straight, logical lines	think in patterns
store data in files and disks	convert learning into experience
use watches, filofaxes and calendars	act when the time is right
think in a calm and cool way	think in an emotional way
like to generalise	deal in concrete specifics
like to learn on their own	like to learn in groups
tend to be very serious	like a good laugh
are on the lookout for new ideas	value traditions, proverbs and customs
learn at the level of theory	learn by doing
collect books	collect beer mats and badges
have a lot of books at home	have a lot of catalogues
have book-lined studies	have workrooms

Are the people you are teaching 'bookish' or 'non-bookish' people? Or both? The answer will determine the style you use in your ministry.

So consider what others need.

3. Decide on what to serve

Sometimes the subject matter of your message is dictated for you in advance of your preparation. Maybe you are part of a team of teachers and you are not the senior leader who chooses the topics or even the texts in your church meetings. Maybe you are a visiting speaker and the people who have invited you have asked you to teach into a particular area and have given you quite a detailed brief, without much chance of flexibility. Or maybe you are speaking in a sermon series, where the menus have already been set and where there is little opportunity for improvisation. If so, the challenge of deciding what to serve is not great.

However, whether the menu is pre-set or not, we will need to hear what the Father is saying before we know what to say and how to say it. In this respect, there is a direct link between revelation and proclamation. The apostle Paul is once again a great example in this regard. In Ephesians 3:3-5 he talks about how God's secret plan was revealed to him personally.

As I briefly mentioned earlier in this letter, God himself revealed his secret plan to me. As you read what I have written, you will understand what I know about this plan regarding Christ. God did not reveal it to previous generations, but now he has revealed it by the Holy Spirit to his holy apostles and prophets.

Here Paul is talking about something revealed to him and others by the Holy Spirit – God's secret plan to include the Gentiles in his work of salvation. Both Gentiles and Jews have an equal share in the riches of Christ's atoning work on the cross. No one could have seen this by human reason. But God has revealed it to Paul by his Holy Spirit.

Paul now turns from revelation to proclamation. What has been revealed to him by the Holy Spirit he makes the subject of his preaching and teaching. So he says in verse 7: 'By God's special favour and mighty power, I have been given the wonderful privilege of serving him by spreading this Good News.' Then in verse 9: 'I was chosen to explain to everyone this plan that God, the Creator of all things, had kept secret from the beginning.'

The key lesson we learn from this part of Ephesians 3 is this: *you cannot say it unless you see it*. Or, to put it more theologically, you can only proclaim with passion what has been revealed to you personally.

In preparing a message, there is therefore no substitute for personal prayer. The person who is called to teach the Bible in the Spirit's power must be a person of prayer. It is only as we spend time listening to the Father in the private place that we will know what to say in the public place. Indeed, an hour of intimate communion with the Father is far better preparation for a sermon than a whole day spent in the commentaries. For this reason, I find it interesting that the apostles in Acts 6 delegated some of their administrative tasks in order to make room for two things: prayer and preaching/teaching. In their own words they say, 'Then we can spend our time in prayer and preaching and teaching the word' (Acts 6:4). Here we see the direct link between spending time in prayerful listening and powerful speaking. The more the apostles had time to pray, the greater the blessing on what they subsequently taught. We need to spend much time in prayer if we are to decide what to serve our people. As John Piper counsels:

> Make your life – especially the life of your study – a life of constant communion with God in prayer. The aroma of God will not linger on a person who does not linger in the presence of God ... We are called to the ministry of the word and *prayer*, because without prayer the God of our studies will be the unfrightening and uninspiring God of insipid academic gamesmanship.

4. Read the recipe carefully

Gertrude Stein once wrote: 'Cookbooks have always intrigued and seduced me. When I was still a dilettante in the kitchen they held my attention, even the dull ones, from cover to cover, the way crime and murder stories did.' A good chef relishes good cookery books. In fact, good chefs rely on good cookbooks. Today, cookery books are back in fashion, not least in North America. As John Thorne, the American food writer, has said: 'Americans, more than any other culture on earth, are cookbook cooks; we learn to make our meals not from any oral tradition, but from a text. The just-wed cook brings to the new household no carefully copied collection of the family's cherished recipes, but a spanking new edition of *Fannie Farmer* or *The Joy of Cooking*.'

Once we have decided what to serve, the next task is a careful examination of what the Bible says on this subject. It may be that you are working to a set text. It may be that you yourself have to find the passage. Whether it is topical or typical exposition (see Chapter 4), you will need to spend time now reading God's word and reading it carefully. As a chef will refer to their cookbook, so a teacher will refer to the Bible. We simply cannot do without the Maker's instructions if we are to be effective.

To show how important this is, I would like to use an example. In my current sermon series on Mark's Gospel, the last passage I spoke on was Mark 11:12–25. This is composed of three paragraphs, the first describing Jesus' cursing of a fig tree, the second, his cleansing of the Temple, the third, his response to the cursing of the fig tree:

(a) *The cursing of the fig tree (Mark 11:12–14)*

The next morning as they were leaving Bethany, Jesus felt hungry. He noticed a fig tree a little way off that was in full leaf, so he went over to see if he could find any figs on it. But there were only leaves because it was too early in the season for fruit. Then Jesus said to the tree, 'May no one ever eat your fruit again!' And the disciples heard him say it.

(b) *The clearing of the Temple (Mark 11:15–19)*

When they arrived back in Jerusalem, Jesus entered the Temple and began to drive out the merchants and their customers. He knocked over the tables of the money changers and the stalls of those selling doves, and he stopped everyone from bringing in merchandise. He taught them, 'The Scriptures declare, "My Temple will be called a place of prayer for all nations," but you have turned it into a den of thieves.'

When the leading priests and teachers of religious law heard what Jesus had done, they began planning how to kill him. But they were afraid of him because the people were so enthusiastic about Jesus' teaching. That evening Jesus and the disciples left the city.

(c) The response to the cursing of the fig tree (Mark 11:20–25)

The next morning as they passed by the fig tree he had cursed, the disciples noticed it was withered from the roots. Peter remembered what Jesus had said to the tree on the previous day and exclaimed, 'Look, Teacher! The fig tree you cursed has withered!' Then Jesus said to the disciples, 'Have faith in God. I assure you that you can say to this mountain, "May God lift you up and throw you into the sea," and your command will be obeyed. All that's required is that you really believe and do not doubt in your heart. Listen to me! You can pray for anything, and if you believe, you will have it. But when you are praying, first forgive anyone against whom you are holding a grudge, so that your Father in heaven will forgive your sins, too.'

The important thing in preparing a message is to let the word of God dictate what you do and say. Be guided by what the text says, much as a cook would be guided by what the cookbook says. As we study the text, the Holy Spirit will start to make certain phrases luminous, and these in turn will form the dominant thought in our sermon.

So, for example, careful study of the first segment of the passage reveals that Jesus hates it when something he expects to be fruitful has no fruit. He expected the fig tree to have at least some fruit. Even though it was not the season for the summer figs, it was the season for the *paggim*, the spring figs. There were usually far fewer of these, but what they lacked in terms of quantity they made up for in terms of quality. These spring figs were the most succulent of all. When Jesus walked up to the tree, he found nothing but leaves. He found the appearance of life but not the reality of life.

Careful study of the second segment shows a similar

theme. Jesus went to the Temple in Jerusalem. The Temple was the very centre of Israel's life and worship. This was where the presence of God could be found. In the Temple precincts there was a huge area known as the Court of the Gentiles. This was a place reserved in God's house for those who were not Jewish. It was a place where Jesus expected to find his fellow Jews praying for the Gentile nations and welcoming non-Jewish pilgrims. When he got there, he found the area had been taken over by people selling doves and exchanging money. Using Old Testament passages, such as Jeremiah 7 and Isaiah 56, he criticised his contemporaries in the most aggressive way. They had turned a place reserved for blessing the lost into a place for blessing themselves. As with the fig tree, so with the Temple; both should have been fruitful. But Jesus found 'nothing but leaves'. So both evoked Jesus' extreme displeasure.

In the third segment, we are back at the fig tree again. It is the next day and the disciples point with amazement at the withered branches. So far in their walk with the Master they have seen only creative miracles. Now they see a destructive miracle and they express their surprise. But Jesus tells them they can move mountains if they have faith in God. Herod had literally moved a mountain to build a fortress for himself just outside Jerusalem. Jesus tells his disciples that they do not need a huge workforce to do great things. They only need faith. We know from elsewhere in the New Testament that without faith it is impossible to please God (Hebrews 11:2). Faith pleases God. So does forgiveness. Jesus says that it is this combination of having faith in God and forgiving others that leads to prevailing prayer. Faith plus forgiveness equals fruitfulness.

Guided by both the word and the Spirit, I began to see that the common link between these three passages was 'what pleases the Lord', and that the key to this is 'fruitfulness'. The Bible tells us that we are to 'find out what is pleasing to the Lord' (Ephesians 5:10). Clearly, being unfruitful does not please him. Clearly, neglecting the lost does not please him. Clearly, relying on our own strength rather than on faith does not please him. As I saw this, I sensed that my message should quite simply be called 'Three ways to please the Lord'. This was the meal I decided to serve, based on a recipe provided by God's book.

So we need to read the recipe carefully. A superficial reading may lead us to making some fundamental errors. This may lead to the whole message being spoilt by a misreading of the original text. Careful study must not be neglected.

5. *Gather all your ingredients*

As you study the recipe of a meal you want to cook, you soon realise what you already have and what you need to acquire. In preparing a meal, you will no doubt go to your fridge, your kitchen cupboards and your pantry to use ingredients that you already possess. At the same time, you may need to go out to the shops or go to a friend to acquire new ingredients. It is just as I wrote in Chapter 4. In preparing a message, we need to bring forth the new as well as the old.

With the passage above (Mark 11:12–25) there was already a fair amount in my larder. I had used it a number of times before and I therefore already knew about the different harvests of figs in Israel, as well as the structure of the Temple. These were old treasures.

When I started to consult the commentaries, I found new treasures. I discovered, for example, that Herod had built a fortress by moving the dirt from one hill to form a high mountain on which to build his fortress. That was new treasure. Consulting a commentary is like going to a shop to buy something new. It blesses you and it blesses your people. Gaps in our knowledge are filled in. In the process, familiar Bible passages are seen in a new light as we are able to explain the meaning of the text in its original context.

But consulting the commentaries is not the only way to gather fresh ingredients for your message. You can also consult with other people. Personally, I feel most Bible teachers are far too individualistic in their sermon preparation. Instead of studying their passage with others, they lock themselves in their study. Instead of dialogue, they prefer monologue. As a result, they miss out on the riches that almost always arise out of studying Scripture in community.

While consulting others, I received a new insight on Mark 11:17. Here, Jesus tells his listeners that they have turned God's house into a den of thieves. A friend of mine, who knows Israel well, informed me that the road up to Jerusalem wound its way through a number of mountainous passes. These mountains contained many caves where crooks used to hang out. From these hidden places, robbers would spring out unexpectedly and mug innocent pilgrims on their way to the Temple. In the light of this snippet of information, my friend explained the full importance of what Jesus meant in Mark 11:17. Effectively, he was saying this: 'You people have travelled here keeping a sharp lookout for robbers' dens. Now that you've arrived, you find that you're in the biggest cave of crooks that exists!'

So we can find fresh ingredients through consulting the commentaries and through listening to others. Another way we can listen to other people is by hearing teaching tapes on the passage of the Bible that we are exegeting. Now, at this point we need to guard against plagiarism. I remember that when I first became a Christian, a lot of my friends copied the most popular Bible teachers of the day. They developed the same mannerisms, the same style of teaching, even the same verbal intonation. We do need to be careful here. Listening to other people's Bible teaching – especially if they are people of the Spirit as well as the word – can be very helpful. It can stimulate you into thinking thoughts that are beyond what the particular teacher is saying. It can, in short, be a springboard to personal revelation. But copying what another teacher has said, both in subject and in style, is wholly wrong. It is not a compliment to God to covet someone else's teaching gift. When the Father created you, he broke the mould.

So, gather your ingredients. This takes time. Devote yourself to an unhurried process of using what you already have and acquiring what you do not. Then let these things simmer together. They will grow richer by virtue of their mutual association. When everything is ready, at the right moment, the message will begin to look like something worth serving!

6. Give care to presentation

Dione Lucas once said, 'The preparation of good food is merely another expression of art, one of the joys of civilised living.' I wholly agree. How a meal is presented is not an optional extra. You may have the finest food on your plate, but if it looks like something better fitted for the dog's bowl it will not appeal. Presenting a meal requires artistic skill.

Three things are necessary if we are to present the truth in a way that is appealing.

The first requirement is *simplicity*. A great message is usually not complex. It is not overcrowded with thoughts or punctuated by Hebrew and Greek. I well remember J. John saying the following in a preaching workshop recently:

> I forget the amount of times I have heard long quotes, flashy statistics and the phrase 'the original Greek word for this is . . .'. But to be honest with you, if I don't hear them again in a sermon I won't be sad, and I'm fluent in Greek! We do not need to parade learning or reading or qualifications.

Precisely. The great thing about Jesus was that he made very deep truths appear extremely simple. This is in fact the mark of a great teacher. Ralph Waldo Emerson made this point when he said, 'The person who can make hard things easy is the educator.' As John Wimber used to say, 'Don't forget the K.I.S.S. principle – Keep It Simple, Stupid.'

On one occasion, my wife and I went to a morning service in a church where the preacher decided to speak on the book of Job. Yes, the whole of the book of Job! She made it her aim to tackle the thorny topic of theodicy – why a good God allows suffering. I remember that when she said the words 'My eighteenth point', Alie and I looked at each other with complete bemusement, scratching our heads, and asking each other, 'Is this a dream?' The remarkable thing about the message was the fact that it was over before the evening service!

When cooking a meal, you are much more likely to

produce something successful if it is simple rather than complicated. 'In cooking, as in all the arts, simplicity is the sign of perfection.' So said a gastronomic genius by the name of Curnonsky. The same goes for Bible teaching. To keep it simple, observe the following two rules:

(a) Keep to one bite-sized portion of Scripture Do not try to tackle a whole book, or even a large chunk of Scripture. A verse, a section, or a short sequence of brief paragraphs is quite sufficient. So, with my message on Mark 11, I chose to focus on three short and clearly related paragraphs. Even though I had the whole chapter to cover, I decided that this was too ambitious. It is always better to focus on covering a small passage really well than a large amount only moderately.

(b) Concentrate on emphasising one main point If you cannot express the aim of your sermon in a single sentence, then it is far too complicated. Once you have your aim, you have your title. In the case of my message on Mark 11:12–25, I gave it the title 'Three ways to please the Lord'. My aim was quite simply to describe three practical things the Lord loves and we all can do.

The second requirement for effective presentation is *structure*. One of the key things about a sermon is to come up with a logical arrangement for your thoughts. T. S. Eliot once said of poetry, 'Organization is necessary, as well as inspiration.' What he meant was this: it is no good a poet having inspired thoughts if he or she is unable to organise them into a coherent form. The same is true of Bible teaching. It is vital to have fire in your preaching, but it is just as vital to have a tidy fireplace in which that fire can burn.

One of the things I have noticed is that sermons tend to gravitate towards one of two ends of a spectrum. At one end, there is 'organisation' or 'structure', and at the other end is 'inspiration' or 'Spirit'. If you listen to most sermons, they are generally one of two sorts. They are either very full of fire but rather lacking in any obvious form, or they are full of form but rather lacking in fire. Yet the most memorable and impacting sermons have both. They are a rich combination of beauty and truth.

The vital thing about structuring your thoughts is to make sure that it is natural, not contrived. We do not impose a structure on a Bible passage. Rather, we discover the structure that the passage actually encourages.

In the case of Mark 11:12–25, this is really very straight-forward. The passage is composed of three parts. In fact, it is an example of what is called a 'Markan sandwich'. In his Gospel, Mark often has three passages that relate to each other by association. The outer passages form the bread, the central passage the filling. Mark 11:12–25 falls into this category, with the first unit about the cursing of the fig tree, the second about the clearing of the Temple, the third about the response to the cursing of the fig tree. The theme that links all of them has to do with bearing fruit.

Now I happen to love sandwiches, so I began my message on this passage by actually bringing into church a packet of my favourite kind, BLT (bacon, lettuce and tomato). I talked about 'Mark's sandwich' and then briefly (and without technical show) about Mark's sandwich effect in his Gospel. I then structured my talk around three points, corresponding to the three parts of the passage:

B = Be fruitful
L = Love seekers
T = Trust God

I used Powerpoint as I went along, so the final point caused a stir of delight in the church as people realised that the talk had the same acrostic as my sandwiches. My BLT sandwiches tasted very good that morning. People seemed to enjoy the message, too. In fact, the amusement caused by the design of the talk helped to make more palatable the strong challenge I was giving to be fruitful in evangelism.

Structure is therefore very important to good presentation. When you go to a really good restaurant, the presentation of your meal is always outstanding. It is well ordered, uncluttered and simple. The same should be true of a good message.

The third and final requirement for good presentation is *seasoning*. A fine meal is always perfectly seasoned by herbs, spices, salt, pepper and so on. In relation to Bible teaching, a message is really perfected by the use of great illustrations. As Howard Crosby once said, 'A wisely chosen illustration is almost essential to fasten the truth upon the ordinary mind, and no teacher can afford to neglect this part of their preparation.'

Where do you find the best illustrations? First of all, from your own experience. There is a call upon the Bible teacher to keep their testimony right up to date. If all we can tell is a story of how we came to know the Lord 20 years ago, then that is not enough. We need to have an ongoing testimony of what the Lord has done in our lives. We need to keep a record of every sign of God working in our ministries. Keeping a journal is a good idea here.

Noting down powerful and encouraging testimonies that our trusted friends relate is also essential. Although we do not preach ourselves, we need to recognise that Bible teaching is a matter of expressing divine truth through human personality. So let us make sure that we actually have a story to tell, and not one that begins 'Once upon a time'.

The second good place to find illustrations is from all around you. Every day, we are confronted by images, experiences and events that could form the raw material of sermon illustrations. The important thing is to be sensitive to the possible connections between earthly realities and heavenly truths. This is precisely what Jesus did when he told his parables. We can do the same. By reading the newspapers, watching the news, keeping in touch with modern movies and the like, we can find fresh and relevant ways to explain the timeless truths of the Bible.

A third way of finding illustrations is through books devoted to this subject. J. John and I have now produced two large volumes of illustrations, jokes, wise one-liners and the like. These are intended for preachers and teachers. The first is called *A Box of Delights*. The second is called *A Bucket of Surprises*. A third is on the way, all published by Monarch. These will give you a huge repertoire of resources to season your sermons and spice up your talks. On top of that, we are publishing three volumes entitled *The Big Picture*. These are collections of messages using modern, mainstream movies to illustrate biblical truths. All three will be published by Authentic. These and many other resources (including websites on the Internet, CD ROMs available through Christian bookstores, as well as other books of illustrations) can provide the help you need.

Seasoning is important. As long as the illustration is truly relevant, it serves the point, and is not too long, then it can be a great way of helping people to learn.

So, work hard at presentation. Remember the three requirements:

SIMPLICITY
STRUCTURE
SEASONING

It really is worth the effort.

7. Serve at the right temperature

This is the final requirement of great cooking. No one wants a melted ice-cream any more than they want a cold tandoori. Sometimes a meal could be hotter. Sometimes it could be colder. The same goes for a message. Here is what John Stott says in his classic book *I Believe in Preaching*:

> Some preachers serve out excellent theology from the pulpit, but it seems to have come out of the freezer. There is no warmth, no glow, no fire. Other pulpits catch fire all right, and threaten to set the church ablaze, but precious little theology goes with it . . .

So what is the solution? How do we get the message at the right temperature? Here is Stott again: 'Once we allow the Holy Spirit his freedom, both in the preparation and in the delivery of our sermons, the light and the fire, the truth and the passion, will again be reunited.'[2] The key is to allow the Holy Spirit the freedom he wants.

---

[2] J. Stott, *I Believe in Preaching* (Hodder & Stoughton, 1988), p. 292.

Sometimes he will want to hold us back and cool us down. At other times he will want to let us loose and set us on fire.

Sometimes he will want us to be more rational and theological. At other times he will want us to be more experiential and anecdotal.

Sometimes he will want us to keep to our prepared notes. At other times he will want us to depart from them.

Sometimes he will want us to preach an entire message. At other times he will want to interrupt us and lead into salvation, healing and deliverance.

It is all up to him.

So let the Holy Spirit have his way in your teaching ministry. Let him determine how the teaching gift is going to be used, to the glory of the name of Jesus.

Question Time

'If the divine creator has taken pains to give us delicious and exquisite things to eat, the least we can do is prepare them well and serve them with ceremony.' (Fernand Point, 1897–1955)

1. How much time do you give to preparing your message? Is it too much, resulting in an over-cooked sermon? Is it too little, resulting in an under-cooked one?
2. Are you in touch with what the people need to hear?
3. Do you listen enough to God?
4. Are you guided by the Bible text?
5. Where do you find fresh insights into Bible passages?
6. Do you talk things through with others?
7. Are you good at keeping things simple?
8. Do you find it easy to express your thoughts logically?
9. Do you record and use effective illustrations?
10. Does the Holy Spirit have complete freedom in your teaching ministry?

Conclusion: Leaving a Legacy

Henry Brook Adams once said, 'A teacher affects eternity; he can never tell where his influence stops.'

If this is true of a schoolteacher, how much more is it true of Jesus? His legacy as a teacher has been inestimable. No teacher, whether in the field of education or religion, has had the impact Jesus has. No other teaching has spanned the great ocean of the centuries with such abiding vitality and relevance as his. Jesus is quite simply the greatest teacher who has ever lived. His message is still changing millions of lives today.

One of the main reasons behind Jesus' matchless influence, besides the divine inspiration behind his words, is the fact that he trained other teachers to pass on his message. Jesus delegated the responsibility of teaching to his disciples. He left them the task of preaching the gospel and teaching his truth. The last words of the Gospel of Matthew, 'the Teacher's Gospel', provide the evidence.

Jesus came and told his disciples, 'I have been given complete authority in heaven and on earth. Therefore, go and make disciples of all the nations, baptizing them in the name of the Father and the Son and the Holy Spirit. *Teach these new disciples to obey all the commands I have given you.* And be sure of this: I am with you always, even to the end of the age.' (My italics)

Here we see how Jesus passed on the baton of the teacher's ministry to his immediate followers. He had invested three years in their personal instruction. Now it was time for them to do the teaching. It was now their responsibility to make disciples and to instruct them.

After giving this Great Commission, Jesus ascended into heaven. Since that day, the church has been called and equipped to continue his ministry here on the earth. In his earthly ministry, Jesus functioned as an apostle, a prophet, an evangelist, a pastor and a teacher: he came as one sent from the Father (apostle); he spoke prophetically into the life of his nation as well as individuals (prophet); he proclaimed the good news that God's reign had begun (evangelist); he acted as a shepherd with those who were harassed and helpless (pastor), and he instructed people in the ways of the kingdom of God (teacher). Now Jesus is in heaven, the body of Christ is called to continue his work until he returns. So Jesus continues to gift people to be apostles, prophets, evangelists, pastors, and teachers. Jesus left a legacy behind him that lasted beyond the lifespan of those standing on the Mount of Olives at his ascension. Jesus' legacy has lasted for 2,000 years because he is still gifting people to do his work today.

It follows from this that one of the greatest responsibilities of the teacher is to follow Jesus' example and to coach others in their gift. Thomas Carruthers once said, 'A teacher is one who makes himself progressively unnecessary.' Elbert Hubbard said that 'the object of teaching a child is to enable them to get along without their teacher'. The apostle Paul clearly had this vision. He said to his pupil Timothy: 'You have heard me teach many things that have been confirmed by many reliable witnesses. Teach these great truths to trustworthy people who are able to pass them on to others' (2 Timothy 2:2). Paul was concerned to train teachers who would in turn train more teachers. His concern was to leave a kingdom legacy.

The call to be a coach

Throughout this book, I have been relying on Ephesians chapter 4 as the foundation for everything I have said. If we go back there now, we will see that those called into the ministries mentioned in verse 11 are called to equip others for works of service (verse 12). I take this to mean that gifted people are supposed to identify other people gifted in similar ways and to pass on what they have learned. As Paul puts it:

> He is the one who gave these gifts to the church: the apostles, the prophets, the evangelists, and the pastors and teachers. Their responsibility is to equip God's people to do his work and build up the church, the body of Christ . . . (Ephesians 4:11–12)

The implication of these verses is a challenging one: apostles are to produce more apostles; prophets are to produce more prophets; evangelists are to produce more evangelists; pastors are to produce more pastors, and teachers are to produce more teachers.

Given that this is the case, mature teachers need to spend time ensuring that they leave a rich legacy. In other words, those of us who have the teaching gift must not only take time to develop our own gifting but also to coach others. Indeed, the best thing for a teacher is not to do the work of twelve teachers but rather put twelve teachers to work – like Jesus did. A true teacher identifies other believers who have the same gift and invests the wealth of their wisdom and experience in those people. Jesus said, 'Freely you have received, freely give' (Matthew 10:8, NIV). If you have received the gift of teaching, make sure you give what you have received to others. As John Wimber always used to say, 'You've *got* to give it away!'

Schools of preaching and teaching

Not long ago, I was speaking with a friend of mine who exercises a prophetic ministry. He has recently set up a training base in the USA. He has established a school of prophecy and runs a three-year programme that covers just about every aspect of the prophetic ministry. It has a clear balance of the word and the Spirit, and is a model of how to coach others in one of the fivefold ministries of Ephesians 4:11.

Last time I was with him, I asked him how many of these prophetic schools there were in the world today. He immediately mentioned a long list of places. I then asked him whether he knew of the existence of any equivalent school of teaching, run by a charismatic church stream or ministry. He thought for a while and then said no – the answer I was sadly expecting. We both agreed that one of the greatest needs today is for schools of teaching which equip believers to communicate the truth of God's word in a Spirit-filled way. While non-charismatics tend to train their teachers very thoroughly, charismatics and Pentecostals have neglected this vital responsibility.

As a response to this, J. John and I decided to start a training school at St Andrew's Church, Chorleywood. J. John's gift is evangelism, so his emphasis is very much on training evangelists to preach the gospel more effectively. My gift is teaching, so my emphasis is very much on training people to teach the Bible in a prophetic way. So far, we have run three years' worth of training days for those who want to develop their preaching and teaching skills. We have invited speakers from all over the world who are people of the word and the Spirit, and they have shared their skills with thousands. Our intention has been to equip evangelists and teachers.

The qualities of a teacher

How do you spot a potential Bible teacher? In helping people to identify whether or not they have a teaching gift, I use Rick Warren's gift assessment tool in his book *The Purpose Driven Church*.[1] Rick Warren is a great teacher and a visionary church leader. He is senior pastor of one of the largest churches in America, Saddleback Community Church in California. Rick believes that God has created each one of us with a unique set of characteristics. Taking his cue from Psalm 139:13–16, Rick talks about the way the Father shaped each one of us in our mother's womb. He uses the word 'shape' as an acrostic:

---

[1] Rick Warren, *The Purpose Driven Church* (Zondervan, 1996).

S = Spiritual gifts
H= Heart
A = Abilities
P = Personality
E = Experience

This is a really good tool for helping people to analyse whether their character and their ministry are in alignment. It is a helpful way of promoting self-discovery and purposeful living.

When I try to assess whether someone is called to a teaching ministry, I start with the person's spiritual gifts (S). Does this person have the gift of teaching? Is there any evidence that the Holy Spirit enables them to communicate biblical truths in a revelatory way? Is there any indication that this person has a calling to an effective Bible teaching ministry? Some people can stand up and speak in front of people but will do so out of their own strength and with their own natural or trained abilities. This is not to be despised, as we shall see in a moment. But the key thing to ask is whether the person has a God-given ability for teaching. If they have, then there will be evidence of it being 'supernaturally natural' for them to teach. It will be a light burden and an easy yoke. If it is a burdensome task, then I would suspect that the person does not have this particular gift, at least not at this stage in their walk with the Lord.

The second thing that needs to be looked at is a person's heart (H). Are they passionate about teaching? Someone who teaches because they think they ought to teach is probably doing the task out of law rather than love. But a really anointed teacher lives and breathes teaching. Bible teaching is their number one passion and priority when it comes to Christian service. They are for ever thinking about the next message they have to give. They are constantly listening to the Father in preparation not just for this message but for every message. They find their greatest levels of fulfilment in actually proclaiming Bible truths and kingdom principles. They communicate with enthusiasm and an obvious liberty. They are most alive in the Lord and most open to the Spirit when exercising their teaching gift. Even at the earliest stage, there will be evidence of some enthusiasm for Bible teaching.

The third thing to look at is a person's abilities (A). Are they actually able to teach? When they open their mouths, do they at least have the potential to proclaim the truth in an inspirational way? Do they have some of the natural aptitudes necessary for effective teaching? Now it is here that we have to be careful. No one begins a ministry of teaching fully equipped for the task. God equips the called rather than calls the equipped. We should always remember this, especially when we are looking at those who are just starting out. Nevertheless, I would expect even the most embryonic Bible teacher to at least have something to say, and have the ability to say it persuasively. If they have nothing to say, I would encourage another ministry. Sober realism is probably the kindest thing here for all concerned. As the novelist George Eliot once said, 'Blessed is the person who, having nothing to say, abstains from giving us wordy evidence of the fact.'

The fourth characteristic to investigate is personality (P). Teaching is the communication of eternal truth through your finite personality. Personality is accordingly important. When I look for potential teachers, I look for the following: a love for God's word, a clear mind, a pastoral heart, a natural enthusiasm, an audible voice, a good sense of humour, a lively character, a physical presence and a sense of integrity. An expert called Albert Mehrabian says words account for only 7 per cent of the total impact of a message; 38 per cent comes from vocal messages – tone of voice, etc. – and a massive 55 per cent is non-verbal, i.e. body language. How a person appears and behaves therefore directly affects what others hear. As Aristotle once said, 'The character of the speaker is their most powerful weapon of persuasion.' We need to remember: nobody ever sold anything by boring them to death.

The final thing to look at is a person's experience (**E**). I happen to believe that everything we face in our lives can be used by God. Nothing we go through is an accident, and no experience is wasted. This applies not only to our lives since becoming a Christian, but also to all that we go through before we are born again. For example, in the years before I gave my life to Christ, I joined a debating society and learnt how to project my voice and to articulate my views publicly. At the time, I did this because I wanted to become a barrister. Looking back, I can see that this was invaluable preparation for a teaching ministry in the church. It gave me some foundational training in the art of communication. After that, I became a school-teacher for a while, before training for the ordained ministry. This experience again was very important in my preparation for the future, especially in learning how to communicate with teenagers.

No experience is wasted in the hands of our sovereign God. A person called to be a Bible teacher will have gone through experiences that have helped to shape them for this privileged role. This applies not only to positive but also to negative experiences. Even our deep wounds can be used to the glory of God in a teaching ministry. In identifying both present and future teachers, we must look at a person's life experiences and ask whether there is anything that looks like the Father's preparation for a teaching ministry. The Father has a long-term investment in the few years we spend here on earth. E. M. Bounds once said, 'Preaching is not the performance of an hour. It is the overflow of a life. It takes twenty years to make a sermon because it takes twenty years to make a preacher.'

The legacy of your life

In the film *Mr Holland's Opus* a music teacher called Holland spends his entire life trying to compose a musical masterpiece. He believes that the composition of such a work would be an indication of his value and the best legacy he could leave. After 30 years of teaching, he is unexpectedly made redundant and told that his job is about to end. He feels dejected and devalued. Having composed his lifelong opus, he is no longer going to have the opportunity to perform it.

On his final day at school, he is brought to the school auditorium where, unknown to him, the students he has taught for over 30 years have gathered to honour him. As he enters, they stand to applaud him. They say to him, 'We are your symphony, Mr Holland. We are the legacy of your life.'

Finally, Holland realises that the true mark of his success was not the composition of his great musical work but rather the people whom he had impacted in 30 years of faithful service. He had spent all that time trying to achieve something great, while not recognising that he was accomplishing so much along the way. On that final day, he does get to conduct his magnum opus, with an orchestra composed of those whom he has taught.

What a lesson this is to all teachers! For those of us called to teach in the church, our greatest legacy will not be a sermon or a sermon series but rather a group of people who have been impacted by our life and input. I doubt whether any of us will ever preach a message that constitutes the last word on a passage of Scripture, or on a particular kingdom principle. But we can coach others to do what we have done, who in turn will coach others, who in turn will coach others. That would be a priceless legacy.

Books and Teaching Tapes

If you are interested in purchasing any of Mark Stibbe's books or teaching tapes, a catalogue can be obtained from:

Word and Spirit Resources Ltd
37 Quickley Lane
Chorleywood
Hertfordshire
WD3 5AE

Other books in the Ministry Guides *series . . .*

The Prophet's Notebook
by Barry Kissell

The first in an exciting new series consisting of five
'Notebooks', each covering a different ministry listed
by Paul in Ephesians 4. *The Prophet's Notebook* will help
prophets to recognise their gifts and use them to build
up the people of God.

The Apostle's Notebook
by Mike Breen

Interest in the apostolic ministry is increasing within
many streams of Christianity. Mike Breen looks at what
the Bible has to say and comes to some surprising and
challenging conclusions on the role of the apostle in
today's church.

The Evangelist's Notebook
by John Peters

If you could look inside the heart and mind of an
evangelist, what might you see? A passion for those
who have yet to discover the love of God in Christ?
But what is an evangelist to make of the church at
a time when so few are being added to it? Can the
inevitable frustration be used in a positive way?

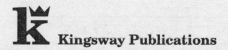 Kingsway Publications

The Reluctant Exorcist

by Ken Gardiner

Ken Gardiner draws on his personal experience and true stories, acquired during 30 years of ministry, to provide guidelines to anyone who feels they should know more about deliverance and related ministries. With common sense and spiritual wisdom he examines such issues as

- distinguishing between mental disorder and demonisation
- possession versus oppression
- how evil spirits can gain access to individuals, including believers
- the cleansing of places
- involvement in the occult, and psychic abilities
- paranormal phenomena, including ghosts and poltergeists
- who or what are demons?

CANON KEN GARDINER has ministered in the area of deliverance for over 30 years. Now retired, he lives in Rochester and still serves on the deliverance ministry advisory board of his local diocese.

MINISTRY GUIDES